Wicca, Druidry
and shamanism

Teresa Moorey

Hodder Education
338 Euston Road, London NW1 3BH.

Hodder Education is an Hachette UK company

First published in UK 2011 by Hodder Education.

This edition published 2011.

Copyright © Teresa Moorey

British Library Cataloguing in Publication Data: a catalogue record for
this title is available from the British Library.

10 9 8 7 6 5 4 3 2 1

The publisher has used its best endeavours to ensure that any website
addresses referred to in this book are correct and active at the time of going
to press. However, the publisher and the author have no responsibility for the
websites and can make no guarantee that a site will remain live or that the
content will remain relevant, decent or appropriate.

The publisher has made every effort to mark as such all words which it
believes to be trademarks. The publisher should also like to make it clear that
the presence of a word in the book, whether marked or unmarked, in no way
affects its legal status as a trademark.

Every reasonable effort has been made by the publisher to trace the copyright
holders of material in this book. Any errors or omissions should be notified in
writing to the publisher, who will endeavour to rectify the situation for any
reprints and future editions.

Hachette UK's policy is to use papers that are natural, renewable
and recyclable products and made from wood grown in sustainable
forests. The logging and manufacturing processes are expected to
conform to the environmental regulations of the country of origin.

www.hoddereducation.co.uk

Typeset by MPS Limited, a Macmillan Company.
Printed in Great Britain by CPI Cox & Wyman, Reading.

Contents

Introduction

Paganism is the fastest-growing religion today. Many of us feel we have lost something radical in modern life. Our traditions are impoverished, our dogmas meaningless and our world robbed of its soul. Pagan paths offer ways of rediscovering our mystic heritage and of worshipping without being required to have literal beliefs and lists of rules.

Pagans happily acknowledge their unrestrained love of life and its pleasures, but they also undertake responsibility, for themselves, humanity and the Earth. There are many types of pagan spirituality, and only a small minority of pagans actually join any tradition. However, to bring paganism to life we shall be examining some of the options in the following pages. Strictly speaking, what we are talking about is Neo-paganism – something that combines the best of the Old in a way that is relevant to what we are today. The word 'pagan', like 'occult' or 'witch' often evokes knee-jerk reactions. This book seeks to clarify the message of beauty, love and respect that is true paganism.

Please use this book as a starting point to explore further for yourself. Delve into myths and meanings. Think for yourself, for life is an exciting journey; you select your own path in your own way. If pagan ways meet your needs, they can open up whole new stretches of country, but this is your own choice. Take your time to reclaim your personal heritage and your links with the Earth, and discover the joy and fulfilment this can yield.

Blessings. Samhain 2011

1

what is a pagan?

Pagans honour the Earth, often seeing her as Mother Goddess, and receiving her gifts with joy and celebration. Feeling a part of all that lives, they treat all with respect. Regaining a sense of roots and ancestry also motivates many pagans. 'Pagan' is derived from the Latin for 'peasant' but today many, if not most, pagans are also city-dwellers.

Paganism is typically non-dogmatic, and pagans may move from one approach to another, or simply follow their own path. Freedom is precious and gurus are rarely sought, for each pagan is a priest or priestess in their own right. Being nature-worshippers, pagans find joy and a sense of belonging in nature. Worship may take the form of rituals, or may just be a matter of attitude – indeed many people are probably pagan without having formally identified themselves in this way!

Who are they?

Pagans are mostly quite ordinary, coming from all walks of life. The popular image of flowing beards, nudity and woodland orgies does not fit the majority of pagans. To be a pagan you do not have to wear special clothes or jewellery, or dance around stone circles. Pagans are found in all types of employment. There are many in the healing professions, for pagans are drawn to healing, and healing the Earth – or at least our attitude to Her – is a pagan vocation.

Pagans do not necessarily deny room to rage, pain, and violence, for these are part of us and part of nature. However, being conscious of these things does not mean rampant indulgence of them – pagans seek the positive in all aspects, and the one rule that is universal is 'Harm none' which is extremely far-reaching. Without winter there is no spring, without rain and grey clouds no blossom. There is anger as well as love, but anger does not destroy love – it can enrich it. Pagans are aware of both sides.

In a sense paganism is a fertility cult and children are treasured and respected. They are brought up to have respect for themselves, for others and for the environment, but they are not forced to believe anything or to participate in anything unless they wish. Pagan parents hope to equip their children to make their own choices, rather than make choices for them. However, pagan families have traditions that focus on the Eight Sabbats, (see Chapter 5), and the idea of living in conscious love of the Earth pervades daily life. There is often a household shrine, and artefacts speaking of a pagan faith in the house, and religious ideas are subtly present in many activities.

Worship and ritual

Pagan worship tends to be about action, rather than belief – about what you do, how you feel, the rhythms of your life, how you participate in the world around you. Some pagans like to write rituals, and most take part in rituals, for through them we find ways to unite ourselves with the natural world. Pagan religious observance is closely connected to the cycles of the Earth, but doing the garden or going for a walk is a form of worship too.

Religion is about inspirations and quests. To a pagan it is mostly the journey that counts, its many meanings and experiences. In the 'Great Mother Charge' (from a Wiccan ceremony) the Goddess tells us: '... thy seeking and yearning shall avail thee not unless thou knowest the mystery: that if that which thou seekest thou findest not within thee thou wilt never find it without thee: for behold, I have been with thee from the beginning and I am that which is attained at the end of desire.' The message here is quite clear: anything worth finding is inside us. It is a mystical thing, and it cannot be communicated or defined. Hard and fast rules are useless on this type of quest.

Above and below

In general the monotheistic, patriarchal religions do not see the body as holy, and by the same token they do not see the world as holy either. Rather, it is there to be exploited; to some even holocaust is acceptable in return for redemption in an afterlife. God is separate from the world and His word is given out by prophets, whose sayings are law. Pagans observe that this is dangerous in more ways than the obvious. It puts power into the hands of people who are not necessarily wise or benevolent and it can even block experience of the divine, for dogma hardly encourages transcendence.

Moreover such an attitude encourages splits — God/Devil, divine/earthly, soul/body, light/dark, man/woman — and such splits often mean that something very valuable ends up cast into shadows and denied. Devil, dark, woman, body, Earth have somehow been thrown together and regarded as an evil package. The pagan way is concerned with deep respect for the feminine in all its aspects. That includes the Crone, menstrual blood, sexual seductiveness and 'irrationality', as well the more generally acceptable faces, such as fecund mother and beautiful maiden. Paganism is Goddess worship, and sexual love is Her gift, there to be enjoyed and valued as sacred.

God and gods

We have seen how important the Goddess is, but pagan ideas about divinity are fluid. It is a question of what inspires or feels suitable at a particular place and time. Pagans do not 'believe in' a God or gods. Their religion is one of immanence, which means that divinity is all around us and within us. It is felt and perceived; there is no act of faith. To some, worship of the Great Mother amounts to almost Goddess monotheism. Many worship the Goddess, in her triple aspect, Maiden Mother and Crone and Her consort the Horned God of Nature, but this leaves room for many other deities from ancient pantheons – and also for gods within tree, stone and river. Some pagans always think in terms of Goddess and God, others always in terms of many, and I suspect most think in different ways at different times. Pagans see no inconsistency in this – it's a question of what works for you. We look at ideas of deity later in our chapter 'Goddess and God'.

It seems that life on Earth is best perpetuated by many different life forms, feeding off each other and dependent on each other in a variety of ways. Pagans see diversity as essential to the spiritual world also. The idea of one path makes it all too easy to destroy institutions, ideas and people. Polytheism can include monotheism, but the reverse is rarely the case. Paganism is extremely tolerant – for instance there are Christian witches. It never seeks converts, and most pagans do not feel they were 'converted' in any way – they simply returned to what they felt most natural, accepted this, reaffirmed it and extended it. There is no concept of sin, although there may be estrangement – from the Earth, nature, or, most importantly, from ourselves. And of course we all have to wear the cloak we weave.

Pagans are united by feeling – a feeling of love, oneness, respect and celebration. Life is more complex than we can understand, and we can extend our reality, our truth, our being by sharing in this. In some ways paganism offers hope for humanity because it trusts us and the essential goodness of us all, regardless of rules and creeds.

If these ideas are new to you, you may like to give them some deep thought. How do you feel about religion without dogma? What might the benefits be? How has dogma affected your life, the lives of your friends, the nations of the world? What is the point of religion to you? And how do you feel about the Earth, nature and the Goddess?

2

the sacred Earth

To pagans nature is holy, and the body is holy. The divine is everywhere, inside us and outside. Our blood and bones were formed from the minerals of the Earth, and to them our bodies will eventually return. Womb and tomb, tomb and womb, the spiral unfolds. This attitude has been passed down to us from ancient time. Our remote ancestors did not build empty shrines to an abstract deity – more probably their worship was about attuning to the energies within the Earth.

This attitude may also afford us an alternative perspective on astrology, because it is quite possible that our sensitive forbears noticed fluctuations first in the energies within the Earth, and related this to movements in the heavens, rather than vice versa. People who lived in close contact with the Earth may have possessed a very different consciousness from the one in which we operate today, and their vision of 'reality' may have been radically different.

Many writers have suggested that the ancients had a very different relationship with the Earth from that which we have today. They worshipped her as Goddess, very practically.

Ley lines

The idea of lines of energy on the Earth, or 'ley lines' was first popularized by Alfred Watkins in *The Old Straight Track*. Ley lines appear to run in straight lines that can be drawn on a map, linking sites of ancient importance, such as churches (which were regularly built in pagans' sacred places) and stone circles. In addition, they often link places with similar names such as Dorrington and Donnington. Perhaps the best-known English ley runs from St Michael's Mount in Cornwall, through Glastonbury and on, to just north of Lowestoft. Leys are also found in Australia. These are the 'Songlines' of the first Ancestors from the Dreamtime as they travelled over the land, singing the world alive. In America there are many straight line features, notably those left by the extinct Miwok Indians in the California sierras. A little investigation of one's surroundings can often reveal much of interest; for instance, ancient tracks used for many years by native people often follow leys.

Places where several leys intersect are held to be areas of power or disturbance: some prehistoric monuments and stone circles were built at such places, and may have been used to contain and increase the current. Some of these intersection points have been the sites of repeated accidents or hauntings. One such place is Windsor Park in England, where Herne the Hunter, horned god of the witches, has been seen several times, and other unusual events have taken place. It seems that the energy disturbance around the leys causes the veil between this world and that of the spirits to tremble and sometimes tear. Interest in ghosts, old buildings and local legends are part of investigating Earth mysteries.

Ley lines warrant serious study in themselves, and many books have been written about them. No one really understands the energy that follows these lines, and some people deny their existence. It is possible to investigate such energies by dowsing, and we shall be looking at this in our Practice section at the end of the chapter.

Seasons and sexuality

The Earth has seasons, and people living far from the equator noticed how the approach and retreat of the sun related to the fertility of their Mother. Many ancient structures mark the cycle of the divine mating of the Earth and sun. For instance, the long barrow at Stoney Littleton in the English Cotswolds is shaped so that every year, for a few moments on Midwinter's day, the sun shines right through to the end of the long passage at the centre of the barrow. This passage has been likened to a vagina, and there is a natural cup mark on a special stone that is illuminated by the penetrating rays. This barrow has many special spiral-shaped fossils, no doubt chosen for their symbolic meaning. Most ancient sites such as this were also burial places, but to suggest that they were merely tombs is as foolish as to say that churches are 'tombs' because bodies are buried there. These places were sacred to the Mother and the dead were returned to the holy Earth, to the tomb that was also womb, so that one day they would be reborn.

Many structures seem to honour the sexuality of Mother Earth. Glastonbury Tor in Somerset looks like a pregnant belly, and Silbury Hill in Wiltshire, erected c 2750 BCE (Before Common Era), has been likened to a breast and a swollen belly.

So we have sites honouring the secret and fertile places of the female body, the body of the Earth, and we have sites linking Earth and sky in celebration. We also have structures to calculate precisely the relationship of the sun, moon, earth and other planets and stars. It seems likely that the ancients perceived links between many things: the sexual and spiritual, life and death, land and sky, the energies within the Earth, and within man himself and the distant stars, from which our ancestors may have come. They may have built their temples of soil and stone to conjure the return of the sun in winter's depth, to access Earth energies, to increase fertility, to ensure rebirth for self and kinsmen or to communicate in some way with people from the stars. It may have been all of these at different times, and more. The ancients probably percieved things that we have lost; they had a holistic perception. Seeing with the eye of the mystic, they lived on a different level, in a different relationship to the Earth. They had direct knowledge of forces that we can no longer appreciate.

Left and right brain

In *The Origin of Consciousness in the Breakdown of the Bicameral Mind* (1976) Julian Jaynes suggests that ancient man possessed a bicameral mind in which the temporal lobes of the brain were interconnected across the anterior commissure between the two hemispheres. So these people would have heard 'voices' like a schizophrenic does and would have been driven to take actions accordingly. The heroes in the Greek myths, he says, heard the 'voices of the Gods' in their heads. It is well known today that the right and left hemispheres of the brain perform different functions. The right brain relates to the left side of the body and (in right-handed people) it thinks intuitively, whereas the left brain thinks logically and relates to the right side of the body. The reverse is true for left-handed people.

Jaynes suggests that the ability to 'hear' voices was lost abruptly by most people at more or less the same time, so people would have felt that the gods had abandoned them. Those who retained the ability to 'hear' would then have been sought out as soothsayers. However, the loss of the voices would have resulted in the desertion of the sacred sites where the skulls of the ancestors housed wisdom, and the voices had spoken most 'ringingly'.

Studies of the brain are continually advancing beyond Jaynes' ideas. However, as a culture we are largely cut off from instinct, inspiration and mystical knowing, although we still possess them. Special sites of antiquity may have the power to revive our split consciousness and give us a vivid experience of the oneness of human, Earth and sky. This is very relevant to the modern pagan, in search of connections with her/his roots and a true experience of the divine in nature – an intense and real participation that makes one know one is 'home'. One of the goals of modern pagans is often to find ways of revitalizing this 'older' knowledge and reconnecting with it.

Many ways may be sought – through trance, dream, shamanic experience or even drugs. However, the best way is to look for this 'knowing' at its source – in Nature herself. Contact with the Earth energies can be made at any place of natural beauty, but numbers of pagans regularly visit ancient sites because these sites are where the power may be most strongly felt.

Developing Earth awareness

Visit ancient sites at times when they are unlikely to be crowded, and go with a relaxed and open mind. Go to enjoy yourself. Take a picnic if you like. Simply notice your surroundings, smells and sounds as well as sights. How is the place affecting your mood? Are you uplifted, pleased – or bored? Pick up any interesting stones or bits of wood you may find – it doesn't matter why they are interesting, don't talk yourself out of anything and don't look for something that's esoteric or symbolic. Be playful. Take a real interest in your locality – buildings, woodlands, local stories, reported hauntings. Investigate where you can.

Get yourself a special notebook to record where you go, how you feel and the dates. After some months of regular visits, either to the same site or different ones you may find a pattern emerges. Don't forget to record the phase of the moon when you visit – this is shown in many diaries and calendars. Is she waxing, full or waning? After a while you may find a connection between the phase and how you feel, for the moon's phases form an energy tide on the Earth, in some ways similar to the effects of her gravity on the seas. If you wish it to be, this notebook can form a record of the development of your Earth awareness. If you live outside the British Isles and there are no obvious sacred sites available, you will have to find ones of your own. Any place that feels special to you is worth exploring.

NB Always use common sense when visiting special sites. Never denude or deface the site or plant life; don't take archaeological remains found with a metal detector (for in so doing you are depriving us all of our heritage); leave no litter, not even the remains of a joss stick.

Practice

One invaluable aid in developing Earth awareness is dowsing. This is more than just a method of finding water with a hazel twig that twitches when a spring is underfoot. It can reveal energy currents, and sometimes the energies are strong in ancient sites. You may dowse with a pendulum. It is best to do this with a small piece of crystal suspended on a chain, that you keep just for this purpose. Simply relax, support your arm and dangle your pendulum over the area. Clockwise movement usually indicates positive energy, anticlockwise negative energy. Programme your pendulum before you start by asking yes/no questions to which you know the answer, and noting in which direction it moves. If the pendulum doesn't move, don't give up. Move to a different location and try again. Anyone can do this. Eventually your pendulum will start to move. Make a note of where and how, and look for patterns.

I'm a recent convert to dowsing rods and these seem easier than a pendulum. You can make dowsing rods from a wire coat hanger. You will need two rods, bent in a right angle, with an upright of about 12 cm, that you hold, and a length of about 27 cm that you poke out in front of you. Hold the short ends loosely in your fists, elbows at your sides, arms bent so your fists are at chest level. You can walk around your chosen site and plot the energy fluctuations. The rods will move — sometimes clockwise, sometimes anticlockwise. Experiment for yourself. Keeping to where the energies are strongest, you can trace lines of energy on the land. Americans may need to be careful, however, for dowsing is illegal in some states, so you may have to rely on developing your instincts. Whatever the case, good hunting!

3

Goddess and God

The idea of the Goddess is very important to pagans and one which arguably sets paganism apart. By honouring the Feminine, new ways can be found to respect the Earth and humanity, and reframe certain rites of passage. The Goddess can inspire women to discover their power, not as surrogate men, but in a more authentic female fashion. She can also inspire men to find their gentle and protective side, and to be creative.

The pagan God is less of a law-giver, more of a Guardian. He is the life-force that surges outwards and impregnates, being gentle, wise, wild and yet protective. He is also lusty, joyful and playful. Pagans have a fluid approach to divinity, sometimes thinking in terms of one creator spirit, and at others of many different deities, within us and outside us. This is not about what is 'true' in some crystallized fashion – it is more about the inspiring and the meaningful.

Forms of the divine

The Goddess is usually seen as synonymous with Mother Earth, and her consort is the Horned God. Belief in a Goddess probably originated with palaeolithic hunter-gathers at a time when the male role in procreation was not appreciated. To many pagans the Goddess is 'first', but this does not mean superior: it is more about the order of thinking. However, some pagans find that a dedication to the Goddess alone is sufficient for spiritual meaning.

An awareness of lunar phases, waxing, full and waning, may have led to the concept of a Triple Goddess, Maiden, Mother and Crone (although some historians believe this is a recent invention). The idea of the God may have come later. He was seen as the embodiment of potency and fertility and yet as the bringer of death and entry into the Hidden. However, this is only part of the story: the pagan view of god-within-matter includes animism, pantheism and polytheism.

Animism means seeing all things as alive. This is the magical world in which stones have personalities and streams speak to us, which tends to be left behind in childhood. Pantheism is the belief that God is everywhere, and amounts almost to the same thing, but with a more pronounced sense of deity. Polytheism means there are many gods, for they are needed to express the lavish miscellany of life. Animism means all is alive, pantheism means all is god and polytheism means many gods. Existence is diverse, the gods are existence and therefore varied. After all, the most fertile ground produces the richest variety of wildflowers, trees, bushes and all the butterflies and bees to flutter and buzz in them. Pagans see religion in the same way.

Pagan pantheons display colourful parades of divinities: joyful, fearful, tragic, funny and often breathtakingly beautiful. They offer us inspiring images that may stimulate creativity in poetry, painting and dance, or may dramatize aspects of ourselves. Myths are often allegories for internal experience and pagans borrow from the Celts, Greeks, Romans and others. Here we look at a few, but anyone interested can look farther, and a quest to find your own goddesses and gods is a true 'magical mystery tour'.

Diana and Aradia

Aradia is especially important to Wiccans, and C. G. Leland's *Aradia, Gospel of the Witches* is one of the key sources of last century's Wicca/witchcraft revival. It tells us: 'Diana was the first created before all creation; in her were all things; out of herself, the first darkness she divided herself; into darkness and light she was divided. Lucifer, her brother and son, herself and her other half, was the light.'

The story continues with details of how Diana fell in love with Lucifer and seduced him, how she became mistress of all sorcery and how her union with her brother produced a daughter, Aradia. Aradia then became her emissary upon Earth, bringing knowledge of witchcraft and hidden arts to the poor and deprived. Aradia says: 'My mother will teach you all things and ye shall be freed from slavery.'

Whether we are enslaved by materialism, dogma, inhibitions or prohibitions, this is an exciting message and Wiccans have preserved it in their ceremonies. Aradia, who is linked to the full moon, brings wisdom, the starlight vision, and freedom – she is a female Messiah. She also represents delight in the pleasures of the flesh and whispers of secret worship in grove and on moonlit hill. Young, beautiful and wise, she is the counterpart of the horned god Cernunnos, a true Nature Goddess of the Witches.

The story of Diana as primal Mother Goddess, giving birth to her son/consort is only one of many from different mythologies and cultures. It is symbolic and certainly does not imply any belief in or respect for incest.

Lucifer (meaning Light) is well known as the archangel who succumbed to pride and was thrown out of heaven to become the Devil. However, the Lucifer in this story is a different matter entirely and no one should infer from it that Wiccans worship the Devil, for they certainly do not; in fact they do not believe in him.

Herne the hunter/Cernunnos

These are the names of the Wiccan Horned God. His horns have many meanings: they are a testimony of animal vitality and potency, they signify crescent moons, and they may represent the fallopian tubes that link the ovaries to the womb. In Shakespeare's time 'wearing the horns' was a sign of the cuckold, a man whose wife was unfaithful. Pagans see this differently, for by identifying with the sexuality of his mate, a man can achieve greater fulfilment for himself and draw closer to the Goddess. The horns are a proud and glorious declaration of revelry in the pleasures of the body. It seems the Horned God was later debased as the Christian Devil, but there is nothing evil about him: he is protective, wise and merry.

The Horned God is the Nature God, eternally slain in bull and stag, yet eternally reborn to be hunted anew. He is also the Hunter, for to identify with his prey, Stone Age man may well have donned a 'crown' of horns, so hunter and hunted became one in a mystical duo.

Cernunnos is the Celtic version of the Horned God, but is probably Latinized, and may have come from the same source as Herne, in British folklore. Herne leads the Wild Hunt across the sky. This is a tempestuous spirit cavalcade, a true personification of lawless nature. There are various legends attached to it, one of which concerns Windsor Great Park, in England, where it is said to appear at times of national crisis. It has also been said that witches used to impersonate the wild hunt to frighten possible captors!

Persephone and Demeter

This is a well-known Greek myth about another mother and daughter duo. It is the story of the rape of innocent Persephone by the underworld god Pluto (Hades to the Greeks). Her mother Demeter is goddess of nature, and after her daughter's abduction she goes into mourning and eternal winter claims the land. All the other gods are disturbed by this and so it is agreed that Persephone will live above ground for half of the year. She cannot leave Pluto's kingdom permanently, because while there she has eaten some pomegranate seeds. For four months she must return to the land of darkness, while her mother mourns anew and winter reigns. Spring comes again when Persephone re-emerges.

Many people now believe that this myth should not be interpreted in terms of female freedom being taken away by male force, or of the seasons being determined by brutal rape. A closer look tells a different tale. The pomegranate is a symbol of fertility, and Pluto, as god of the land beneath the earth, is in a sense sent by the Great Mother herself. Astrologically Pluto rules the 'feminine' sign of Scorpio, and is associated with power, sexuality, death, rebirth and transformation. What takes Persephone by storm is the onset of mature sexuality, for sexuality brings direct experience of the awesome power of nature as it manifests in tempest, earthquake and tropical sun. It also has links with karma. Sexuality is knowledge, knowledge is power – Persephone becomes Queen of the Underworld – and power means change.

Persephone is also called Kore, and her worship was important in the rites of Eleusis, the mystery cult. This is a myth of many meanings, one of which is initiation, which means entry into a new understanding – a concept worthy of our consideration.

Pan

The 'goat-foot god' exemplifies nature at its wildest and most unpredictable, and indeed he is another horned god. One of the myths about Pan concerns his love for the nymph Syrinx, who, in common with most of his lovers found him a bit much. The river god who was Syrinx's father turned her into a reed to save her from him. Pan – obviously a pragmatist – plucked the reed and made his Pan-pipes. This is a haunting tale of loss inspiring creativity, and of participation. Pan does not walk away in mourning from the riverside; nor does he pick the reed and set it on a shrine. Instead he makes something of it. The story has a lot to tell us about how to deal with frustration, and about connecting with nature and truth.

The word 'panic' derives from his name, and may be allied to that strange and overwhelming fear that can take possession when we are totally alone with nature, on a mountain or deserted moor. This is no human fear. The very soil murmurs of a primeval power that hardly notices our existence. However, in psychotheraputic terms panic and hysteria can have their roots in disconnection from feeling. Fear of nature can be a result of feeling separated from her. Mysticism is one way of reuniting. Working up a healthy sweat through a hard slog up a hill, or simply putting palms to the earth can work too. Chaotic and orgiastic, Pan tells us to surrender to the natural in order to understand better, to feel better.

Pan also means 'all', which perhaps implies that Pan is omnipresent. Plutarch tells the story of a sailor passing the Echinades Islands at the time Christianity was beginning to take over much of the known world. This sailor heard a voice crying 'Great Pan is dead'. To pagans that has a poignant ring. However, Great Pan is now very much reincarnated, and he represents the 'all-ness' without dogma that somehow unites pagans across the globe.

Isis

This Egyptian goddess, whose worship spread far afield, has been described as the most complete goddess form that has evolved. Her very name evokes the archetypal Feminine. She and her husband Osiris ruled Egypt and taught mankind the skills of civilization, but their brother Set became jealous and killed Osiris. However, Isis searched for all the parts of the dismembered body, and magically conceived a child, the god Horus, from her dead husband. Osiris became king of the Underworld, but he is really one of many dying and resurrecting vegetation gods, reborn as his son Horus.

So Isis was the faithful wife and mother who understood suffering. She was also goddess of magic and healing, in which she was helped by Thoth, god of wisdom, showing that true feeling allied to understanding is the basis of magical endeavour. Thoth was married to Ma'at, who represents the inescapable order of the cosmos – yet another factor for the magician/witch striving to act in harmony with Nature and to understand it better.

Mercury/Hermes

Hermes was the messenger of the Olympian gods, called Mercury by the Romans and pictured wearing winged sandals.

He was the god of intellect, and of travel and trade. One of his most important functions was to lead dead souls into Hades, and in that he was unique for very few could enter the dark realms and return. This suggests the way in that intellect can lead us to hidden wisdom. He was also something of a trickster, being patron of thieves, and he had many lovers – there has even been a suggestion that his identity is not strictly masculine, and that he is more androgynous. As an intellectual deity he would be associated with the element of Air, which is considered a 'masculine' element – however that perspective may actually be considered old-fashioned.

Mercury carries a staff, called a caduceus, around which serpents are entwined. Serpents represent wisdom and sexuality, among other meanings, so this is no simple god. As the father of Pan he represents the cerebral leading to the instinctual. Conversely, the instinctual may be a valid path to understanding.

Cerridwen

This is a Welsh goddess, well known for her cauldron of inspiration and rebirth, from which the bodies of dead heroes emerged, healed and alive. Often she is seen as the Dark Mother, the tomb that swallows, and one of her symbols was the sow. She had a hideous son called Afagddu, which means Darkness, and for him she prepared a brew of wisdom. However, a few drops of this spilt onto little Gwion, whom she asked to stir it, and he sucked the splashes and received the gift of wisdom. There follows a chase in which Cerridwen and Gwion assume many different animal forms until at last he becomes a grain of wheat and she becomes a hen and eats him. Subsequently she gives birth to a beautiful boy who is the bard Taliesin, of legendary fame. The message from this is that from death comes life, from darkness comes beauty, and from the unnameable comes wisdom. It is an initiation story.

Lugh

This is the Irish sun god, or god of light – his name means 'shining one'. He was also god of many crafts. He is celebrated especially at Lughnasadh, or Lammas, the festival at the beginning of August. At this time the god is cut down and is reborn in the bread made from the harvest grains, so identifying with the sun, which 'dies' and 'resurrects' in temperate latitudes. Because of this he can also be seen as a vegetation god, for plants come and go with the sun.

Brigid/Bride

Bride (pronounced *Breed*) is the great mother goddess of Ireland, and is often seen as a form of the Triple Goddess. She was widely worshipped and was particularly goddess of fire, smithcraft, healing, childbirth and poetic inspiration. As St Bridget, she is beloved of the Irish, who have made many wells sacred to her. It seems that expanding Christianity turned as many heathen customs as possible into Christian ones, and Bride survived as Ireland's favourite female saint. The symbol for Bridget is the woven Bridget's cross, which is a type of cross where the four arms meet to form a square centre and opposite arms are parallel but do not form a straight line. This can be seen as a fire wheel, but it is also like a swastika. The cross has many meanings which have nothing to do with Christianity, and the swastika has occult significance that pre-dates the Nazis by centuries. One of the interpretations of the swastika is that it consists of four gammas, or Greek 'g's (the Russian 'g' is similar) and so is the initial of Gaia, the Greek Earth Mother written four times, so meaning fecundity.

The Green Man

I include the Green Man here because he seems quintessentially pagan. His image is found on many churches as the 'foliate mask' – a face made up of leaves. The Green Man is also embodied in the Green Knight of Arthurian legend. The Green Knight represents nature, and more specifically the Holly King, or King of the Waning Year, from midsummer to Yule, while Gawain was the Oak King of the Waxing Year. Barely even human, he has a vegetation face, sometimes benevolent yet strangely remorseless. He appears in church architecture, perhaps placed there by masons who weren't as Christian as they pretended. Along with the Sheil-na-Gig, the hag with the yawning vulva, also found in churches (notably at Kilpeck Church, in Herefordshire), he is a reminder of the ineradicability of pagan feeling, and he can be seen each time we are in woods and look up at the sunlight through a roof of woven leaves.

Practice

We have examined a small number of goddesses and gods, but most areas of human life are represented. Are you undergoing deep and unsettling changes? Persephone or Cerridwen can help. Do you need clear thought for a project, interview or exam? This is Mercury's province. If you need help in love, call on great Isis. Perhaps you need help in creative endeavours, conception, childbirth: put this in the hands of Brigid. Need healing, energy, freedom from care? Call on Cernunnos or the Green Man. Pan is best left to his work of attending nature, for his energies are unpredictable.

Settle yourself quietly, out of doors if possible, in a place where you will feel safe and will not be interrupted. Still your mind and allow a feeling of peace to bathe you. Close your eyes and visualize the god or goddess of your need approaching you, tell him or her your trouble and put it in her/his hands. Allow yourself to feel consoled and optimistic. The Great Ones are there to help humans. When you have finished, thank your god/dess, take a deep breath and open your eyes. Place your palms on the ground for a few seconds to earth yourself. Make a small offering to the deity – perhaps some food or wine placed upon the earth, and know that your pleas will be attended to.

Perhaps you would like to choose one of the familiar pantheons, Celts, Graeco-Roman or Egyptian and explore further for yourself. What gods or goddesses really inspire you? And why?

4

witchcraft and Wicca

Witchcraft is a religion of nature worship that usually celebrates the seasonal cycle in eight festivals or 'Sabbats'. In these the mysteries of birth, death, sex, growth and decay are honoured. In some ways witchcraft is a fertility cult. Today we may not be so concerned about crops and livestock, but with other creative meanings. Our dependence on the Earth is as real as ever, and needs to be affirmed. Witches also worship the God, consort of the Goddess, and are inspired by many ancient myths from Celtic, through Greek and Egyptian. Witchcraft is both a tradition and a magical system.

Many pagans perform magic of a sort, because this seems to arise from closeness to natural forces, and is really a form of positive thinking. Rituals still the conscious mind, to allow the older wisdom of the unconscious to come through. Magic can raise consciousness and is most often used for healing.

There is some confusion about the terms 'Wiccan' and 'witch', so for simplicity I will divide witches into four main types.

Traditional

Some witches call themselves 'traditional' because they follow ways that have been passed down through the family. However, it also seems that much 'traditional' witchcraft is less of a religion and more a set of customs that may not be called witchcraft by those who follow them – times of persecution would doubtless have had an effect. Also, some traditions are secret.

Hedge witches

These are lone witches, who usually celebrate the eight Sabbats and each Full Moon, following a path similar to Wicca, but more spontaneous. Variations may be immense, as solo witches are often visionary, poetical and interested in self-development. They are not bound by any rules except 'harm none' which is almost universal. Solo witches are often called 'hedge witches', but there is a trend, especially in America, to call lone witchcraft 'Wicca'. Witches of this sort are often motivated by visions and glean information from books. They initiate or 'dedicate' themselves when they wish, usually practise magic, have no degree system, keep their own records, or not, as they wish, and may honour the Goddess more strongly, or possibly the God.

Open-style craft

There are less formal groupings of witches, who also work alone. They have many other names, such as Kitchen Magic, Folk Magic, the Craft or Weavers. Although they may not see themselves as part of the same group, there are many similarities. They are independent and may be feminist. Sometimes there may be a defined leader, usually a priestess, or a couple. Sometimes they form groups/covens or circles but tend to be informal about it and also work alone. There is an emphasis on personal development, intuition, shamanic techniques, practical crafts, ecology and healing. It is this more open style which has created courses, public festivals and a developing sense of pagan community and available services.

Wiccans

These have a defined system of initiation and group in covens under a High Priestess and High Priest. It is a mystery tradition that follows definite rules for festivals and rituals, celebrating eight yearly Sabbats, and Esbats usually at Full Moon. Wiccans also call themselves 'witches' and Wicca is often referred to as 'the Craft'. Wicca has existed in its present form since the 1940s and rites and ceremonies are recorded in a 'Book of Shadows' and may be copied down by initiates as part of their training.

In practice these four types can overlap a great deal and none is really more authentic than the other. However, to give a starting-point, the following concentrates on Wicca, as it is currently the most structured form.

Being also a magical system, Wiccan rites take place within a magic circle. This is a circle created by visualization and ritual, that exists on the spirit plane and offers protection and containment. Covens do magic at the Sabbats, or at other times. At no time is anything intended to harm, for the one rule that Wiccans and witches follow regarding all activity – not just magical – is 'If it harms none, do what you will'.

Wiccan covens are not self-development groups, but ways are offered to expand as a person. Training nights are an important routine, and one is expected to be discreet about the identity of other members. Wicca is a mystery religion akin to those of much earlier times and there are secrets that are not shared with outsiders. The details of initiation rites are not discussed in advance and this can make the experience more powerful. However, the real mystery is what happens inside, which is incommunicable. Rites can unlock hidden depths and bring about an inner change, even if what happens outwardly is less than majestic. The transcendent is approached through the body, not by denying it – the pagan approach – and so Wiccans usually regard having fun as important. Feasting is part of the process and coven members will often bring food to enjoy after the ritual.

The High Priestess is really the coven leader. She is 'first among equals' but that should not mean 'superior' in the usual sense. Goddess-worship and the full development of female potential are very basic to the ideals of the Craft. Rites are often conducted 'sky-clad' which means in the nude, but sexual exploitation is absolutely forbidden and no one under 18 is initiated.

First of all, newcomers are accepted into covens as 'neophytes' or novices. As they progress they are initiated into the First Degree. This is followed by the Second and Third Degree, after which they are regarded as being in a position to leave, form their own covens and initiate others. Initiation involves certain vows of support, but these are not binding in any compulsive fashion. Covens can really be of any number that remains sufficiently cosy and each initiate is considered to be Priestess or Priest of the Goddess – no one has the exclusive hotline to the divine. Covens are not cults and anyone may leave when they wish. However, it is common sense to approach any new group of people with care and ensure that you feel comfortable before committing yourself. Wiccans do not seek converts for there is nothing evangelical about the religion. In Wicca the focus is, to a great extent, the Sacred Marriage of Goddess and God. Following on from this, Druidry emphasizes the birth of the Divine Child. There are many connections between the two paths that are being rediscovered by present-day pagans.

The history of Wicca

Wiccans feel their ancestry begins back in the days of standing stone and tumulus, when the great Earth Mother was universally worshipped. By 500 BCE the Celts had become a major force in Europe. Women were powerful in their society. They have passed down to us the four main festivals of Imbolc, Beltane, Lammas and Samhain that we shall be looking at later.

European influences

Two strands of thought from Europe were also influential. The cult of Apollo emphasized philosophy, consciousness and solar rites (Apollo was a Sun god). On the other hand the Dionysian approach was one of ecstasy, trance and merging – more a province of the grove than the temple. Dionysus was god of wine and has been associated with the intuitive water sign, Pisces. Both of these ways were to some extent combined in the mystery cults of Isis and Eleusis, which aimed to raise consciousness through philosophy and inspirational experience.

Persecution

Mostly the ancient gods lived comfortably side by side until Christianity appeared, proclaiming itself the one and only truth and stamping out competition with a savage ruthlessness on the part of some churchmen. The old religions disappeared or went underground. Then the Renaissance saw a growth in ritual magic, which in a sense was a revival of the Apollonian approach. However, these magicians had rites that called upon an ostentatious array of saints so they mostly evaded persecution. Magicians were often influential men.

The Dionysian strand lived on in village witches, and it was upon these that the inquisition and anyone else who wanted a scapegoat or an excuse to steal property, concentrated. Most of its victims were women, and there may have been as many as 9 million of them, throughout the Middle Ages. Witches were tortured horrifically and burnt at the stake – alive, if they refused to admit what their captors wished – which must have put many unfortunates in a no-win situation. After the Reformation this was illegal in England (but not in Scotland) and witches were hanged instead. It is said that the persecutors would not have caught a real witch, but this is uncertain. Any 'real' witches would have scented trouble a mile off, but escape may not always have been practical.

Easier times approached and interest in the occult grew in the nineteenth century, which also produced a work by Charles Leland called *Aradia, or The Gospel of the Witches* (the Vangelo). Leland was a charismatic and urbane man who gained entry to societies normally suspicious of outsiders. *Aradia* tells of secret rites to the Goddess Diana and Aradia, her daughter: this was called the Old Religion, and had been handed down through many centuries. The Vangelo forms the basis of some of the Wiccan rites of today and Wicca/witchcraft is still called the Old Religion.

Next came the lively and well-travelled Margaret Murray, an anthropologist and Egyptologist whose studies revealed the existence of an extensive witch-cult and the involvement of the English monarchy in this. In the early twentieth century she published *The Witch Cult in Western Europe, The God of the Witches* and later *The Divine King in England*.

Gerald Gardner, who may be regarded as the founder of modern Wicca, was initiated into a traditional witch coven in the New Forest. He is also said to have had connections with an East Anglian coven of a similar nature, led by a colourful 'cunning man' called George Pickingill. Gardner was heavily criticized for publicizing witchcraft but he said he wished to make it available to younger people who could revitalize the old ways and pass them on.

Aleister Crowley, better known as 'the Beast' and sometimes thought of as a black magician, also had links with Pickingill. Crowley was probably a tormented character, whose habits (such as relieving himself upon the floor of his hostess's lounge!) suggest he had more than a little of the rebellious toddler about him. His evil reputation is not really justified, and he coined some wise sayings, notably 'Do what thou wilt shall be the whole of the law; Love is the Law, Love under Will'. The 'True Will' is not the desires of the ego, and the role of love is supportive, not subordinate.

The last historical figure was Alex Sanders, whose initiation history is obscure. His grandmother may have introduced him into traditional witchcraft, or he may have entered a Gardnerian coven. At all events, the strand of Wicca that we know today as 'Alexandrian' comes from him, whereas the 'Gardnerian' originates with Gerald Gardner. The differences between them are not extreme and we shall not be concerning ourselves with them here.

This is the story of modern Wicca, originating in an unbroken line from the Stone Age, through the Celts and Greeks, surviving underground in cults and covens through the 'Burning Times'. It was resurrected almost intact by recent scholars, and tidied up by Gerald Gardner and Alex Sanders to be practised by us today.

Myth and history

However, almost everything written about above has been contested, some of it very hotly. Leland was a satirist and the *Vangelo* has been called a hoax. Margaret Murray has been called a deluded old woman and Gardner has been accused of borrowing wildly from every source under the sun. Some say there never was a universal Goddess worship and the 'witch-cult' was an invention of a Church that wanted scapegoats. So what are we to believe?

The truth is probably somewhere in between. There may never have been universal Goddess worship but there have been more female figures unearthed in digs than male ones, and it seems women undoubtedly held real power in Celtic society. As for the Middle Ages, it seems true that the patriarchal organization of the Church, influenced by the woman-hating St Paul, denied space to many things that are considered feminine – the instinctual, the non-rational and indeed the naturally physical. It also called evil any form of worship other than its own. Life in those times was very hard. Goddess worship, far from condemning bodily enjoyment as sinful, actually regarded it as a divine gift. It seems reasonable that this, along with such things as ecstatic experience and herbal lore, may have been secretly preserved by the common people, mostly in a disorganized form, and sometimes called by other names than 'witchcraft'.

Further, Margaret Murray appears to have been a lucid and scholarly lady and Leland a sensitive and poetical man. There seems little reason for him to invent the *Vangelo* and in any case the mixed mythology that it contains is rather what one would expect of a doctrine kept secretly alive for many years by an illiterate and oppressed peasantry. In respect of Gerald Gardner and Alex Sanders, regardless of their origins the contribution they have made is undeniable and inspiring. If Wiccans and witches have to invent stories – and many do – perhaps it is an indictment of our society that intuitive people feel they have to invent 'authentic' sources to be accepted.

All this is useful because it is the Wiccan 'myth' and has been much debated. Whatever may be true, what we practise now cannot be the same as the ancient ways of cave, grove and stone circle. Nor should it be, for we and our needs are very different from our ancestors. The literal truth is not really important, especially to pagans, because paganism is not about doctrine or dogma, but what fires the imagination, frees the soul and brings the kinship of the heart. Witchcraft is a way of beauty and inspiration, where there is poetry in leaf and stone, wisdom in the hills and freedom for the spirit, where the Old Ones walk with us and each small pleasure is a festival. Most people initiated as Wiccans or witches feel they have come home. It is a feeling of comfort but also of a strange and terrible awe. For what we come 'home' to is very old indeed – older even than humanity itself.

Practice

Go out by yourself into a forest or lonely field and try to imagine what it was like to be a poor person in medieval times, or before. There is no central heating to shield you from winter's blast. Your crops are at the mercy of the weather and inconvenient rain could mean a long, hungry time for yourself and those you care for. If you break a leg on the way home there will be no anaesthetic or welcoming hospital to help you.

What might your ideas about the gods be? To whom would you turn for help? What might you do to feel better about life, more hopeful? Make a note of all thoughts, however far-fetched they may seem.

5

cycles and celebrations

Most pagans mark the turning seasons in some way – they are a metaphor for our lives and an affirmation of our closeness to the Earth. This can be humbling, but also uplifting, because it gives us a sense of being part of something greater than ourselves – which is arguably what spirituality is all about. Rituals, celebrations and folk customs mark this, and it may be all the more welcome to pagans who live in cities and who feel 'uprooted'.

In ancient pagan cultures there were several levels of involvement in ritual observance. Folk customs and superstitions may have been observed by the ordinary folk, but there were also esoteric disciplines, such as the Eleusinian Mysteries. Honouring the seasons helps us to honour the process of growth and change within ourselves, and this cyclicity has been respected since ancient times, carved in spiral symbols on stones, wood and cave walls.

Seasonal customs

Here we shall look at some folk customs that are mainly British, although the true meaning of the times and seasons can only be discovered by inward journeys, and is quite incommunicable. It is worth noting that only the 'minor' mysteries of Eleusis were secret. The inner mystery, which is about union with the divine, was not secret. This is because it cannot be told – only experienced. The best way to approach this is first to get as much contact with the natural world as you can. This is so easily overlooked in quests for something arcane. Secondly, practise trance/visualization.

The Wheel of the Year

The seasonal cycle is often depicted as a wheel with eight spokes or segments, for there are eight Sabbats or festivals in all, and the circle turns perpetually, one season leading to another, growth followed by maturity, decay and death, then producing new life again. Each part of the cycle is linked to a direction, an element, a stage in the evolution of the story of the Goddess and God, with other special gods and goddesses, and with totem animals. We can see the Goddess as the Wheel itself – the process of life – and the God as Son/Sun travelling around it. There is more than one version of the Wheel of the Year (sometimes called The Medicine Wheel) and this is explored at length by Kathy Jones in *Spinning the Wheel of Ana* (Ariadne, 1994). The best idea is to construct your own 'Wheel of the Year' and enter the feelings and associations that are important to you. As you begin to explore these ideas and attune yourself to the cycle you will find your understanding of the subject will deepen.

The cycle starts with Samhain (pronounced *sa-ween*) On 31 October, which is also called Hallowe'en, and this is believed by some to be the Celtic New Year. The Goddess is present as Wise Crone, the God is Lord of the Underworld. Then at the Winter Solstice or Yule (22 Dec) the Goddess as Great Mother gives birth to the God anew, as the Divine Child. At Imbolc (2 Feb) we celebrate especially the inspiration of the Goddess as Maiden, but also as Mother, for She has recently given birth. At the Spring Equinox (21 March) both Goddess and God are youthful. The Maiden Goddess is bright with potential and in the greenwood the God grows to maturity. At Beltane (30 April) the Goddess and God mate and celebrate their sexuality. At Midsummer (22 June) the Goddess and God both glow with fulfilment of their union. The Goddess gives birth to nature, and again at harvest time, Lammas, (31 July) She gives birth to the grain and fruits. Then at the Autumn Equinox (21 Sept) again we celebrate the last of the harvest. The God is cut down with the corn at Lammas, and He is reborn, in a sense, in the loaves and produce made from the harvest, in another sense He begins a journey to the Underworld, to reign as Lord of Death at Samhain, and to be born again at Yule. This is all told from the perspective of the Northern Hemisphere, however. Many Australians prefer to 'rotate' the Wheel, marking Beltane at the start of November, Yule in the middle of the year, and so on.

Of course, this cycle is full of paradox and contradiction. The Goddess and God are within us always, but we focus on different aspects of them for a more vivid experience at different times. The God is seen as dying and reborn, but the Goddess is envisioned as changing Her face. In addition to the 'story' given above there is another aspect to the God cycle – that of the Holly King and Oak King. The Holly King is King of the Waning Year, as the Sun fades from Midsummer to Yule. He and the Oak King battle at Midsummer, and the Holly King wins. They battle again at Yule, and the Oak King is victorious. The Oak King rules the Waxing Year, from Yule to Midsummer. Holly and Oak represent the light and dark sides, but dark does not mean evil. It signifies things that are quiet, hidden, perhaps necessarily destructive, but containing wisdom. It is important to pagans to honour darkness as well as light, for that way is balanced, and not repressed.

Also, to understand the Goddess more fully we need to remember that She is Triple – Maiden, Mother and Crone, and each of these three aspects is equally valuable. Some pagans see the cycle in terms of the Goddess alone, some include the God, as Wiccans do. You can explore your own ideas of Goddess and God, and also the many personifications which we looked at briefly in Chapter 3. The Goddess can be Great Mother, She can be Triple Goddess, or She can appear in a hundred different ways as Venus, Freya, Morrigan or Brigit. Similarly the God can be young/old, light/dark or He can come in the guise of Herne the Hunter, Osiris or Odin. In short, it is what works for you that is important.

Samhain (31 October)

Mists creep in early, leaves fall, nights grow longer. This is an eerie time when the veil between us and the world of the spirits is thin. Ghosts – and witches – walk abroad, and we remember the Ancestors, both recent and from the distant past. The Christian festival of All Souls' Day is on 2 November. 'Samhain' is usually taken to mean 'summer's end' but this is the start of a fresh cycle. We sweep up leaves, prune and cut – and plant bulbs to grow in the spring.

The best-known symbol of Hallowe'en is the pumpkin, hollowed out, with a candle shining through its grinning mask. This is the face of the Crone, She Who Watches. The native turnip lantern was also used to frighten away spirits by those who walked out into the night. Another meaning is that in the darkness light continues, hidden in tubers, seeds, dormant under the earth but still glowing, like the candle in the pumpkin. Besides this, Samhain is a time to think about masks – like the lantern face. We all wear them, showing faces to the world that are only an aspect of our true selves, and at this time of transformation we may like to change our mask/s or even dare to drop them altogether for a while. A mask is not just a disguise however – it can also be an invocation. Wearing the correct mask can call forth aspects of ourselves, from deep within. A similar idea can be the wearing of an animal skin – we can wear a bearskin to draw out the fierce 'bear' from inside us.

So the simple Hallowe'en lantern has lots of meanings, like most things. A pumpkin lantern is easy to make, for the inside is usually quite soft. Swedes and turnips are more traditionally British, but they are harder to hollow and carve. Cut a piece out of the top of the pumpkin, with the stalk at the centre. Make sure this is reasonably large, for you'll need to be able to get your hand down it. Then you can scoop out the seeds with your hands and hollow the inside out with a fairly sharp spoon. Some pumpkins require a fair bit of hollowing to be thin enough to cut the face; others hardly need any at all, but you will probably want to remove the threads the seeds were attached to. Draw a face on the outside (you can buy kits for this) and cut through with a small, sharp knife. If the eyes, nose and mouth are big enough there will be enough oxygen to keep the candle alight when the 'hat' is put back on. Put the pumpkin, complete with candle inside in your window and wait for the Trick or Treaters.

Trick or Treat seems to have arisen in the United States – but it is a revival of older, similar customs from Europe. Children dressed as vampires and ghouls knock at doors demanding a 'treat' and if one is not forthcoming – beware!

This has been criticized for a variety of reasons, but basically it seems very healthy. Boundaries are down now, and the spirit of the season is honoured by the 'trickers'. We are not all sweetness and light and neither is nature. It is better to acknowledge this symbolically by a bit of harmless fun than to deny it.

For the Celts, Samhain was the start of the story-telling season. In our family we mark this by telling ghost/horror stories by candlelight. Each person holds the fort for a specified time, usually two minutes, as any longer can be hard for children. When time is up the next person takes over, and it is interesting how the emphasis of the story shifts, from the gothic graveyards-and-white-sheets of the youngsters, through macabre teenage humour to a more subtle adult approach. The atmosphere is lifted by someone's funny ending, lights go on and it's supper-time.

Apple-bobbing is a favourite game at Hallowe'en parties. Although ruled by Venus, the apple is associated with the Crone and with Underworld knowledge and wisdom. Cut an apple crossways and you will see a star shape at the centre – the five-point star shape is sacred to the Goddess. The apple must be pulled out of the water with your teeth. The animal instinct is foremost, human hands must not be used, and if you end up with your head under water that could mean the waters of the unconscious overwhelming a mind that has become too sophisticated. A little beer or cider will help!

The major festivals of Samhain, Imbolc, Beltane and Lammas are believed to be older in origin, arising from herding cultures, whereas the later agrarian people became more concerned with the exact position of the sun at the equinoxes and solstices. These were fire festivals and sometimes human sacrifice may have been practised. Often it would have been the king who willingly died, as the God 'dies'. It has been said that human sacrifice was a later, patriarchal innovation and that the older matrifocal societies did not practise it. No one can be sure. Nowadays it is a horrifying thought, but it's interesting that in Britain we have our bonfires on 5 November to burn not a king, but the would-be king-slayer, Guy Fawkes.

The purpose of Samhain ritual is to create an atmosphere where the spirit world feels close enough to be tangible. Also we wish to honour the forces of death, for it is death that gives life its purpose and decay that fertilizes new growth. Sex, added to birth and death, forms a trio of transformation. Fertility is honoured at Samhain in the nuts and fruits we may gather, but there is a side to sexuality that has little to do with procreation and far more to do with the experience sexual passion can give us of darker parts of our personality, its role in deep transformation and connection with spirituality and karma. This is also remembered. The Sun is now in Scorpio, water sign of passion and transformation. The element of water is connected with feeling and remembering, and Scorpio is ruled by Pluto, dark lord of the Underworld.

Yule (22 December)

This is the depth of winter, and some traditions interpret this as a time of death, but it is also birth, for at this point the Sun begins to make the return journey. All of our well-known Christmas customs celebrate the return of light in some way, the power of the birth-giving Goddess and the advent of the Magical Child, the

Sun/Son God. Many religions mark the birth of a divine child, at some point.

If we look behind the dogmas and outer trappings, in truth we all worship the same god/dess. At Yule the brotherhood of man is remembered in the Christmas spirit and the message of love and new birth.

At Christmas, which comes three days after Yule, we exchange presents. These are our gifts for the Divine Child, as all new babies are showered with gifts. It is often said that Christmas is a 'time for children', and especially it is a time for the child of the Goddess, the bright Sun that now begins to grow in strength.

Father Christmas is a well-known figure. He is reminiscent of the witches' Horned God, Herne/Cernunnos, with his horned reindeer. Also his hearty laugh and rosy cheeks suggest the Oak King, whose reign now begins again. The merry Horned God was debased as the Christian Devil, who is also called 'Old Nick', and Father Christmas is also called Saint Nicholas, or Saint Nick. He may also have developed from the German goddess Holda, who dressed in red and came down the chimney with gifts. Coca-Cola advertising developed our current Santa image, but his essence is far older.

Evergreen trees are sacred to the Goddess, for they retain their greenery all year round. Almost everyone has a Christmas tree, decorated with brilliant baubles that catch the light and seem to conjure the return of the Sun. On the top of the tree we place our Christmas Fairy – yet another Goddess image, to honour the birth-giving Mother. We also decorate our homes with holly (for the departing Holly King) and mistletoe. Some say mistletoe is sacred to the Sun, but I prefer the Moon as ruler, for the berries are moon-white and their juice is like semen, which is ruled by the Moon. The seventeenth-century herbalist Culpeper says that mistletoe is best grown on the oak – so mistletoe is for the Oak King. We kiss underneath it for fertility and happiness.

Other winter customs are Mumming Plays and pantomimes: merry slapsticks that celebrate the seasonal spirit. Wassailing – a noisy ceremony to drive away harm from apple trees – is a local tradition in apple-growing English counties. The Roman Saturnalia took place at this season, and was a time of role-reversal and generally 'letting it all hang out'. The Sun enters Capricorn, Earth sign of the goat. The goat is a great climber, and the Sun now climbs in the sky. Capricorn is ruled by Saturn: although known for discipline, there is another side to Capricorn that is lusty, well-deserving of the goat's horns and quite at home in the wildness of Saturnalia.

In Wiccan covens, two male coven members are usually chosen to act as Holly King and Oak King, and they enact a symbolic struggle, which is won by the Oak King, of course. The ritual emphasizes the return and rebirth of the Sun and of the God.

Imbolc (2 February)

Days are lengthening and although the weather may be cold we are aware that life is definitely stirring. White snowdrops dance in the sharp wind and ewe's milk flows with the birth of the lambs. The Sun is now in the sign of the Water-Bearer, Aquarius, which is an air sign bringing the waters of enlightenment at this festival of Light.

At Imbolc the accent is on the Goddess, both as Mother (She gave birth to the Sun God about six weeks ago, and all mothers will be familiar with the 'six weeks check-up') and as inspirational Maid. Imbolc is the Feast of the Poets, when we celebrate the flame of creativity. The goddess Brigit is especially honoured at this time: originally she was a form of the Triple Goddess. One of the customs associated with Imbolc is the making of a Bridie Doll by dressing up a sheaf of oats in women's clothing and later placing it in the earth. This has links with fertility rites. The women of Glastonbury in Somerset have developed this beautifully.

There is another lovely custom associated with the Bridie Doll. She can travel around to different houses and then returns to base to be put in a sacred Bed. Each woman then takes it in turns to share her Bed and to tell of feelings and experiences about motherhood and birth – youngest first. Meanwhile the men toast the Goddess at the pub and are given a right royal welcome when they return for the final feast. A woman could do this on her own, with her own special Bridie doll, dreaming or meditating about mothering and anything related, and perhaps writing down thoughts or poetry if she wishes. Make your own Bridie Doll if you like – it doesn't matter how amateurish you feel your efforts are. This is a good time for men to renew commitment to the Goddess.

The Roman Feast of Lupercalia, which took place on 15 February, was sacred to Pan. It was a time of unruly fertility ceremony and cleansing. St Valentine's day (14 February) is when couples declare their love – 'coming clean' and hoping for fulfilment. 'Lupercalia' derives partly from *lupus* – Latin for wolf. Sacred to Brigit are the wild wolf, wise snake, the fertile cow and the far-sighted bird of prey. You may like to consider these creatures and what they mean for us at this time of awakening, and to think of new beginnings and creative projects.

Rituals at this time are about the re-emergence of life and a celebration of the Triple Goddess.

Spring Equinox (21 March)

The Sun now enters the fire sign Aries, sign of the impetuous Ram. Light and dark are in balance but light is gaining. Life is now establishing itself in the spring flowers and longer days. Easter, named after the goddess Eostre, the Teutonic Maid goddess of the Earth, is calculated by the Moon, occurring on the first Sunday after the first Full Moon after the Equinox. We are familiar with Easter's Christian theme of sacrificial death and resurrection, and this echoes similar pagan traditions of sacrificial gods that die and resurrect like the Sun does yearly. In our spring-cleaning we make way for the new, and it is a good idea also to do this inwardly.

Hot cross buns are traditional Good Friday fare. The cross has many meanings and this equal-armed Celtic cross means the four elements or directions, the four seasons and is really a Wheel of the Year itself.

The hare links several strands of myth. Sacred to the Moon Goddess, witches were thought to shape-shift into hares. The hare has been known as a self-sacrificing animal, so maybe connected with the sacrificial god. Rabbits acquire some of the hare's mystery. The Easter Bunny is a symbol of fertility, said to bring the Easter eggs, and eggs of course are a metaphor for the life that is 'hatching' everywhere now.

When I was small it was the 'bells', not the Easter bunny, who brought the Easter eggs. In this European tradition, the bells returned to Rome after their silence during Lent, dropping eggs on their way. Bells are also a much older symbol. Their round shape makes them special to the Goddess and their ringing often marks significant points in rituals.

Eggs can be decorated for friends and family at this time. Use food colouring, and plenty of imagination.

The wheel is an important symbol for Wiccans at this festival, meaning the circle of the seasons in perfect balance (also echoing the Hot Cross Buns). The theme of the festival is the Sun's growth in power.

Beltane (30 April)

This has been called the oldest and most important festival, for nature is riotous and blooming and everyone feels the stirrings of vitality and sexuality. The Sun is in Taurus, an Earth sign ruled by Venus and known for its sensuality. The best-known symbol of Beltane is the maypole – a phallic pole planted deep in the receptive earth. To wash your face in the early morning dew of May Day was believed to guarantee continuing youth and beauty.

As people danced around the maypole, holding the ribbons that trailed from the top, the winding and unwinding of the spiral of life was enacted. Dowsers (see Chapter 2) can sometimes detect patterns of energy where the dancers trod. One of the tallest maypoles now standing is in the village of Paganhill – appropriately named – near Stroud in Gloucestershire. It is painted red, white and blue – very patriotic colours, but they are also the colours of the Triple Goddess. White is for the Maiden, red for the Mother and blue (though more usually black) for the Crone. This is yet another example of hidden pagan meanings. The Puritans were alive to the sexual symbolism of the maypole and it was banned, but Charles II reintroduced it during the Restoration.

The custom of going 'A-Maying' meant staying out all night to gather hawthorn, watching the sun rise and no doubt making love in the greenwood – the so-called 'greenwood marriage'. Mark this festival by gathering hawthorn yourself if you wish. There are many merry customs all over Europe to celebrate this time, with dancing, flowers, music and processions. In many places a young girl is crowned as May Queen, and this has links with Maid Marion of English folk legend. Maid Marion is really the Maiden herself, greenwood goddess of the deer, the hare, the secret and the fertile places of the forest. Her consort Robin Hood is also the Green Man, or Pan – the spirit of lawless nature himself.

The cross-quarter festivals were all celebrated by bonfires. Cattle were driven between two fires at Beltane for luck and a good milk yield. As with other festivals the indoor substitute for the Belfire is a candle in the cauldron. Beltane is named after the Celtic god Bel, the 'bright one'.

Rituals now emphasize sexual allure and the joy of healthy sensuality. Celebrate with a party, excursion or barbecue – whatever feels right for you.

Midsummer (22 June)

The Sun is at the height of his powers, although June is not the warmest month in Britain. Now we celebrate the very peak of summer and the things we have brought to fruition, remembering that as this point is reached, so begins the inevitable journey back into darkness. As everything in the world of vegetation seems to be coming to full fruition the Sun enters the nurturing water sign of Cancer. A woman who wishes to conceive should walk naked through her vegetable garden on Midsummer's Eve, preferably picking some St John's Wort. This is a solar herb that flowers at this time. Among other things it is said to be effective against melancholy and madness – so explain that to the neighbours if they spot you!

The great stone circle of Stonehenge is now subject to restricted entry. There are probably many reasons for the construction of this majestic temple of stone and winds, the Giant's Dance. On Midsummer's Day the Sun rises directly over the Hele Stone. The ancients probably were more deeply attuned to the rhythms of land and sky and the penetrating solar rays represented the divine meeting of Earth and Sun. This is the Druid feast of Alban Heruin, 'The Light of the Shore', their most complex ceremony, preceded by an all night vigil round the solstice fire. The Dawn Ceremony used to be performed at Stonehenge before it was banned – rather like banning the Pope from the Vatican! However, Druids are now pre-admitted to stonehenge. You may like to have your own dawn vigil, going to a special high place and watching the Sun come up, if the weather is clear.

On a lighter note, this is the time of year for Morris Dances in Britain. The Morris Men (or 'Mary's Men' as some scholars have suggested) dance in honour of the Goddess, waving the white handkerchiefs of the Maid, their bells, ribbons and ribaldry strongly suggesting fertility rites – a repeating theme. In the United States, 4 July is Independence Day – a significant time to proclaim liberty. Shan reminds us that this is a time of large gatherings, so go to a pop concert, cricket match or even Wimbledon.

Rituals emphasize the power of the Sun and the glory of summer flowers. This is a festival of water as well as fire, which were both seen by the ancients as transformative. The Sun is now in the water sign of Cancer, setting sail for the south. The drama of the Holly King and the Oak King are enacted in some way by Wiccans, with Holly winning this time, as the year begins to wane.

Lughnasadh (31 July)

This means 'Feast of Lugh' and is pronounced *Loo-nus-ah*. Lugh was god of fire and light to the Celts. Another perhaps more usual name for this festival is Lammas, meaning 'loaf-mass'.

Now the air is heavy with fruitfulness and the Sun seems to have come to Earth. Lammas/Lughnasadh takes place between the hay and grain harvests, but really it marks the start of the harvesting proper for most produce is gathered in between now and the Autumn Equinox. It is a time to think of the harvests in our own lives, too.

A phenomenon often seen especially in the Wiltshire fields is the crop circle – stalks bent in perfect circular shapes, that are often quite complex. Some of these may be hoaxes, but whether this is the case or not, these circles are a reminder of the spiral of life and the relationship of crops to ancient powers of Sun and soil. Some people try sleeping in the centre of these circles and the resulting dreams are sometimes vivid and meaningful.

Perhaps the best-known seasonal custom at this time is the making of the Corn Dolly. The best ears from the last sheaf cut would be taken and made into a corn dolly, which was generally kept over the hearth for good fortune. The seeds were then shaken out and sown with the new seeds the following spring. The traditional colour for tying or dressing the Corn Dolly is red – colour of life and the Earth Mother. You can make your own simple Corn Dolly from a few ears of wheat, but just take a few from the edge of the field out of respect for the farmer.

This is a festival of life, in the harvest, but also loss, for the Corn Spirit is cut down, and the Sun begins to 'die'. Please note, the British meaning of 'corn' is usually wheat, and nothing like the corn-on-the-cob that may be more familiar in the States.

The focus of ritual now is to celebrate the harvest and to mark the death – and life – of the God. We mark the positive aspects of sacrifice. Now is a good time to make a pledge to do something specific for the Earth – perhaps planting a tree.

Autumn Equinox (21 September)

As at the Spring Equinox light and dark are in balance, but now dark is gaining. The last of the harvests have now been gathered and thanks can be said for the successful completion. The Sun enters Libra, air sign of balance and peace. There is a sense of shifting gear as life prepares to retreat and we think about what we must put to one side as winter advances.

This was the time of the Eleusinian Mysteries, about which we know little for the initiates kept the secrets closely guarded. However, it seems that some of the rituals centred upon the descent of Persephone/Kore to the Underworld, to reign as Queen until summer. This is not hard to interpret: only by going within and facing darkness, both in ourselves and the coming winter, are we able to obey the Eleusinian instruction, 'Know thyself'.

The obvious custom is making preserves, jams and chutneys from the seasonal produce which I have always done 'religiously'. Now in Britain it is time to gather blackberries from the hedgerows. There is nothing like the satisfaction of making blackberry pie from your very own 'harvest': you may like to have your own 'harvest supper' to give thanks for the bounty of the earth.

Wiccan rituals centre upon a single ear of wheat, which echoes the climax (it is said) of the Eleusinian ritual where the initiate was shown an ear of wheat and told, 'In silence is the seed of wisdom gained'.

Moon observance

The rhythms of the Moon are at least as important as those of the Sun. While the Sun is linked to consciousness and reasoning the Moon is associated with the unconscious, and regarded as 'feminine'. Instinct and femininity are close to the hearts of the pagans generally. Earth is the body of the Goddess, but the gleaming Moon, waxing as Maiden, Full as Mother and waning as Crone is Her celestial manifestation. The Moon rules menstruation and the tides of life. Her phases are said to affect the growth of plants, the incidence of accidents, bleeding from wounds, and entry to mental hospitals. She also rules the entry into the Mysteries of self-knowledge, body-knowledge and spiritual experiences.

As mistress of magic and starlight vision, the Moon is very important to solo witches who may choose to mark her phases with a variety of rituals and activities. Wiccan non-festival meetings are called Esbats and these are traditionally held at Full Moon. A beautiful Wiccan ceremony is that of 'Drawing Down the Moon' – also done as part of the opening ritual to Sabbats.

Lunar rhythms are important to our lives and often neglected. You may like to make them a part of your life by simply noting the day of Full Moon and buying a bottle of wine to toast our Mother in her glory. Try lighting a candle – perhaps a red one, for that is the colour associated with the Mother, but any colour you like will do – to mark this special time. Full Moon is a good time to meditate on our wild and instinctual side.

Practice

This chapter has given you many seasonal things to do. Begin by thinking about the next festival to come and listing all the things about it that come to your mind, both personal and general.

Make your own 'Wheel of the Year'. Don't be afraid to enter your own associations, even if you don't know what they mean – meanings may become clearer at a later date.

With the Moon, begin by noting her phases in your diary, taking moonlit walks and noticing how your energy grows, reduces, is applied in different ways, and how your emotions fluctuate with the phases.

shamanism

Our image of the capering medicine man is very far from New Agers seeking enlightenment in jeans and funky waistcoats, and yet shamanism is bringing revelation and vivid experience to many people today, as we seek our own, personal connection with the transcendent. So much of paganism is orientated towards *experience* rather than *belief* and this is particularly apparent when we embark on shamanic journeying.

This chapter describes a particular sort of shamanic experience. However, many pagan paths have an element of shamanism within them, and while a lot of the symbolism and mythology for shamanism is derived from Native American culture, shamanism may well have been practised world-wide in ancient times. Today it certainly informs the attitude of many witches and Druids. As with so many paths, there is much in shamanism that helps with the personal development on which we concentrate today. However, underlying this is the ever-present link with the world around us, and its hidden essence.

A shamanic experience

In a session in a shamanic lodge about 30 people, all interested in subjects that can be called esoteric, gather together to hear a talk on shamanism, and find out for themselves. They are grouped in a circle, two deep. In the centre the guides for the evening set out a Medicine Wheel, based on symbolism from the Lakota tradition. (There are about 400 different tribes in North America, all with their own variations on the Wheel and its symbols.) 'Medicine' means power, and the power symbols are placed at the four compass points, arranged on a circular mat. This is very similar to the witches' circle although there is a difference in the association between elements and quarters.

The circle represents the cycle of life. The east is the place of morning, of spirit, fire and spring. It is a doorway, a seed-place, a pre-embryonic stage. In the east of the circle are grouped yellow stones, seeds and flowers and a spiral symbolic of the coil of life. The colour of the east is yellow.

The south is the home of the Plant Kingdom, of the flowers and abundance. It is associated with midheaven, midday, summer. Its element is water and its colour is red. Here are grouped brilliant flowers and red stones.

The west is the home of darkness and eventide. Its element is Earth. It is associated with the mineral kingdom, and with harvest, and its colour is black. Here are grouped various dark artefacts, black and grey stones, and also a bear, for bears have an affinity with west.

In the north are grouped various animal figures, for north is linked to the animal kingdom, to winter and to midnight, to the pitch-black time when nature holds her breath. The element associated with north is air.

The slice of the wheel that feels most appropriate to us says something about our essence or our need. For instance, if someone needs to 'sit in the south' it means they need a bit of warmth and passion in their life. But the wheel isn't a strict map of shamanic journey. Like many pagan ideas, thinking of the wheel helps our sense of connection and it is a basis for action and movement, not a creed. It is also beautiful, and the way of the shaman is a path of beauty, a path of balance. The shaman lives in this world, as poet, mystic, wounded healer, but he journeys into the Otherworld and finds inspiration. In a way there is no such thing as a shaman – he is undefinable, he exists in his actions, in his experience. Yet we are to explore something of what it means to be a shaman.

The guides tell the group they are going on an inward journey to find their Power Animal – an animal that symbolizes an energy that is helpful to us and we can learn to access. The fragrance of burning sage and sweet grass fills the air. The candles are lit, the lights go out. Everyone takes a deep breath, closes their eyes and relaxes. Now they imagine simply that they are sitting in a pleasant field. The journey starts as the drum begins to beat.

After this each person's experience is personal, and may be colourful, revealing, dramatic or boring! At the end of the session experiences are shared and sometimes interpreted by other group members and often surprising animals have been encountered.

Shamanism – where, what and when

The Medicine Wheel described above is part of the tradition of the American Indians. This is a living tradition, by which I mean it is part of the life and culture of the people, and their daily framework. As neo-pagans and witches we tend to live only partially in terms of our spiritual visions, and some of us split off our paganism from segments of our life, either because others wouldn't find it acceptable, or possibly because we just can't keep it up. So we feel a nostalgia about cultures where there is integration. However, there is something distasteful about stealing traditions from a people already dispossessed in other ways and certainly many Native Americans feel rightly incensed at the way some people never initiated into their ways presume to teach their traditions. As this book is about neo-paganism, not about traditions that can claim a completely unbroken line down hundreds of years, this will be our only look at the American Indian. Borrowing is different from stealing, however. The image of the Medicine Wheel is a colourful loan from the most accessible living tradition today, and that is why it is so compelling.

The Amerindians are certainly not the only culture to produce shamanism. *Shaman* is a Siberian Tungusic word meaning 'ecstatic one' (*ex-stasis* from the Greek, meaning altered states of consciousness) and forms of shamanism are, or were, found in North and South America, among Australian Aborigines, in Indonesia, China, Tibet and notably Siberia itself. It is arguable that most races at one time in their history had persons who could enter the spirit world and return with valuable information for the tribe. There is a shamanic thread in witchcraft, which claims archaic lineage, and trances can be induced in various ways, by dancing, chanting or by learning to shift consciousness by a mixture of relaxation and visualization.

The shaman is distinct from a medium, 'channeller' or the ancient Delphic oracle, for instead of the spirit taking over, the role of the shaman is essentially an active one. Shamanic journeys seem almost always to have had a purpose – to discover the origin of problems that may beset the people, such as lack of food or sickness, to help departed or tormented souls or to understand the nature of the breaching of tribal taboos. Unlike the medium, who has no recollection of the spirits who have taken over her or him, the shaman comes back from his journey with a clear memory and precise instructions.

The practice of shamanism is based on the belief that reality has many levels, and the universe consists of a complex energy-network of powers, vibrations and forms, of which the shaman gains direct experience. Most cosmologies used by shamans include three worlds: upper, middle and lower. Usually humans inhabit the middle world, and the three may be linked by a great tree, a sacred river or a road. In Norse mythology the World Tree Yggdrasil grows from the lower world Hel, through Midgard and into the realms of the gods Asgard. For the Siberian Evenks, the three worlds are linked by the Clan River that rises in the upper world where the creator god Amaka lives, also Eksheri, the master of animals, birds and fish, whose good will was needed for good hunting. The lower world is the domain of the dead clansmen, the spirits of disease and of the Clan Mistress, who rules the hunt. The Clan Mistress is half animal, half human, and although the lower world is less pleasant than the upper it is the place of roots, and totemic clan unity stems from there. To become whole we have to seek integration with our darker side and with the things we fear, and the key to full living is strangely hidden in the cave of our deepest terrors. It seems that the shaman would often perform this function of journeying to the forbidden and fearful for the whole tribe, and come back with valuable information for hunt and health.

Although to be a shaman was in a sense a privileged position, it was not usually sought. Rather it seized one, and often arose from a threatening experience such as sickness, assault or a 'near-death' experience. The assumption of the shamanic role was a form of healing, which sounds like a positive use of a disability – the 'wounded healer' archetype. Because of his wounds, his openings to another world, the shaman had access to levels of reality denied to those more whole. Shamanic journeys were dangerous, involving magical dismemberment and rebirth, and possibly one might not return from the spiritual world. Shamans were often helped by spirit guides such as animals or deceased shamans. They were also under potential threat of psychic injury by shamans from opposing tribes, who might be more powerful.

Shamans have been credited in folklore with the power to shape-shift, to go forth in the form of an animal, as witches and sorcerers have been reputed to do. However, in Siberia where the word originated, this was apparently not the case. Accounts of this possibly come from the shamanic ability to merge identity with an animal, or have animal spirit helpers. Drugs were sometimes used by shamans to induce trance states – notably the peyote and San Pedro cacti in South America – and the use of these dates back many thousands of years. There is also the Fly Agaric mushroom that grows over many northern lands. However, it was mostly believed in Siberia that a shaman who needed drugs to go into a trance was second rate. Shamans are by no means always men. In recent history there were often female ones, and there are those who argue that shamanism is most naturally the province of women, and in earlier times when women held more power the shamans were almost always women. A myth of how men long ago stole power from women is told in some variation in all shamanic cultures. The feminine form, *shamanka* is sometimes used.

Shamanism today

Shamanism today has a few things in common with the harrowing journeys of the tribal shaman.

However, it must still be remembered that the shamanic journey has a function, for example to find a power animal. There can be several power animals for one person, and it may take several journeys to find them. Discovering them increases a sense of effectuality, and you may surround yourself with images of your power animals to help you in specific situations.

Workshops, courses and groups that operate today are for the purpose of self-discovery, development and enlightenment, and to enable us to do that magic thing – re-connect. Finding that way of living in harmony with the Earth and taking care of Her is so necessary to our well-being. So these journeys do not serve the purpose of ensuring survival of individuals or tribes, but they do keep the vision alive of who we are and where we are going, and the responsibility for the modern shaman is essentially the same: the health and Spirit of the people.

Finding your power animal

As you start on your shamanic exploration, a short visualization of a 'journey' to meet your power animal can be helpful and revealing. If this is your first time, please do not expect much in the way of results. Lie down and relax. If you have a tape of drumming music, play this, for the drum was the shaman's 'horse' and the drumbeat can help to change your consciousness.

Let yourself enter a 'day-dreamy' consciousness. Imagine that you are wearing a protective travelling-cloak. Now, in your mind's eye, take yourself to a special place out in nature. Take time to get used to your surroundings. You may start to notice that this place, although familiar, is not quite like the one you know. Perhaps the colours are more vivid. Perhaps you glimpse spirit beings there. Ask that your power animal come to meet you.

After a while you should find an animal comes to you. Remember that *all* animals have their special gifts and the whole point of journeying is to find what you *really* need, as opposed to what you *think* you need! You may rather like the idea of Panther, while Frog may not seem so glamorous! However, be respectful to any animal that approaches, for you will be honoured and benefited by it.

Some animals may come close but not approach you. Wait until an animal comes up to you and challenge it, 'Do you come in peace and love?' Remind yourself that you have your protective magical cloak around you. Ask this three times – any creature that means less than well will evaporate. One that stays is your champion.

Journeying with your animal

Meeting your power animal may be journey enough for the first few tries. Ask your animal questions if you wish – it may seem as if your animal speaks to you, it may show you something or the answers may appear in your head. Sooner or later your animal will want to lead you on a journey. Before following, make sure that you feel ready for the experience. If you don't there will always be another opportunity.

When you are ready, just follow your animal. You may find that you experience the countryside more as if you were that animal, rather than in your human form. Speak to any beings you may encounter – all this has a message for you.

At some point you will know it's time to return – either because you want to or because your animal signals it's time to go. Make sure you return to your starting point, thank your animal, and say goodbye. Take off your travelling cloak and come back to the here-and-now. Write down your experiences in a special journal – often the meanings of things become clearer with hindsight.

And remember – if you have another question, or something is not clear – journey again! In time you will find it becomes easier and your experiences become more vivid.

7

Druidry

Roman historians speak of Druids, yet there is controversy over the details. Through years of repression it seems pagan ways went 'underground' and it is hard for anyone to claim unbroken lineage back to the Stone Age! However, Druidry fares better than witchcraft in that respect, because in some ways it has been more cerebral, and many respected men have been 'Druids' – notably William Blake and Winston Churchill. These days Druids are also women.

After a period when the association of Druids with stone circles such as Avebury and Stonehenge was considered apocryphal, we are now told that early Druids did worship there.

However, this does not really matter, for Druidry is about connecting with the Druid spirit, which is alive, and building bridges of understanding and awareness. Any association with human sacrifice is unfair – this was practised in ancient times for various reasons, and the Druids were no more guilty than others. The most likely meaning of Druid is 'Wise man of the oak', and like all pagan paths, Druidry forms a connection with the beauty, power and essential harmony that is nature.

Levels of Druidry

Training to be a Druid took a long time and I am tempted to believe that many of our forefathers, in days when life expectancy was much less than it is now, must have died in the attempt. There were three levels of Druids – Bards, Ovates and Druids themselves.

Bards

The Bards were the first grade and working through this could take up to 12 years, after which the student would know hundreds of poems by heart. Bards kept alive the traditions of the tribe in song and composed their own poems – but these were seen as much more than entertainment or historical record. Whoever said 'Sticks and stones may break my bones but words could never hurt me' was insensitive and blind to the evocative power of words to arouse emotions, recall and organize concepts for the memory and understanding, evoke, heal, clarify and command. Words are vibrations and they possess powers that we cannot fully encompass with the logical mind. Poetry and music break down the barriers that consciousness constructs, easing the loneliness of the soul and showing us that we are all one, that we are part of the rolling hills, the tumbling stream and the ancient yew tree. These are values from which we have become estranged, to our cost.

Although placed as the first grade, the Bardic grade lay at the heart of Druidry, for the Bards were masters of creativity. In *The Druid Tradition* Philip Carr-Gomm tells us, 'The Bard's knowledge of and skill with the power of the Word becomes magical with the Druid: understanding the creative force of sound, the Word is used to generate seeds of light that echo through creation.' The Bardic grade is represented by the birch tree and associated with spring and dawn.

Ovates

The second grade was that of the Ovate. Here the initiate learned not only to open the doors of perception, achieved by the Bard, but also those of time itself, and these are shamanic practices. The Ovates were seers, prophets and diviners, working in the realms of death and the spirits of the Ancestors. The lore of trees and herbs was the province of the Ovate, for contact with the plant kingdom connects us to the mysteries of time, death, transformation, sacrifice and rebirth. Plants have many healing properties which the Ovate would have known about, but their more general healing power is what we need to rediscover today – for they show us a way to find connection with the roots of our own beings and find that elusive but simple oneness with nature. The tree of the Ovate grade is the yew, and it is associated with autumn, winter and night – times of reflection and assimilation.

Druids

The third grade was that of the Druid himself. Having made his way through the long and arduous training and having honed his creative powers and his memory and extended his consciousness, the Druid was able to act as judge, philosopher, adviser and teacher. The tree representing the Druid is the oak, and associated with this grade is the east and the times of greatest light and growth – noon and summer. Now, for the Druid the spiral begins anew, reborn through the Bardic Grade and progressing around and upwards, obeying the injunction 'Generate and Regenerate' for life is an ever-growing and changing process and the Druid is both of the ether and of the earth. Concerned with and connected to his environment but fired also by the spirit, the Druid represents much that is relevant to our needs today.

Druids traditionally observe the Eight Festivals. For a Druid the Wheel of the Year and all it tells us about our lives and place on the Earth, in nature and the cosmos and the Wheel of Rebirth is as significant as it is to most pagans.

Druidry honours the spirits of the Ancestors as these are the roots from which we have sprung. It also honours the influence of past lives, for though we may not recall them, the memory is lodged in the Unconscious and has links with current experiences we have. This memory is the Spirit of the Journey. Some people seem able to cope with the most dreadful early circumstances and find meaning and purpose in their lives, while others struggle with comparatively minor troubles. These differences can be explained to some extent by the Spirit of the Journey working through the current life. Druids also honour the Spirit of Place – the Earth is sacred and certain places are special. There is a quality to Place that is much more than co-ordinates on a map, and feeling a sense of this helps us feel we have a 'place' in the scheme of things. Finally there is the Spirit of Time that we honour when we observe the round of the seasons and the motions of the Moon.

For rituals witches draw a magic circle, invoking the protection of the powers of earth, air, fire and water at the north, east, south and west, in that order. The five Spirits of the Circle of the Druids (Ancestors, Unconscious, Journey, Place and Time, as described above) could be linked as follows: Spirit of Place with earth/north; Spirit of the Tribe with east/air (air being connected to the spoken word, and thus to tribal lore), Spirit of Time to the south/fire (where we see the movements of Sun and Moon in the Northern Hemisphere), and Spirit of the Ancestors to west/water (realm of setting Sun, Isles of the Blessed Dead, Waters of healing, remembering, connecting). Thus the Spirit of the journey related to the fifth element, ether, or spirit, that transforms and enlivens from within. You may like to play with other associations and discover meanings for yourself.

Druids have been linked to stone circles, and this is allied to their respect for the Spirit of Place, for these are erected at places of special power on the earth's crust (see Chapter 2). Besides this, the astronomical calculations inbuilt into such structures were important for Druid observances – the truth is 'written in the stones' and there is far more 'truth' here than can be appreciated by measuring and reasoning. However, the Druids are also seen as teaching in groves of sacred trees, and tree lore is significant in Druidry.

Tree lore

Ogham

We have seen how knowledge of plants was required for the Ovate grade. The Druids built up an extensive system of associations or 'correspondences' connected to trees, called Ogham, and it seems this was as complex and rich as the mystical doctrine of the Qabalah. Each tree was associated with a letter, number, god/dess, mineral, bird, colour, star and so on. This way of thinking about things is very enriching and it seems to bring the world to life, provoking all sorts of ideas, symbols, poetry and inspiration and is a tremendous aid to memory. At first glance it may seem somewhat mechanical, but in practice this is not so at all – it opens up the world and doors to different levels of experience in a way that has to be put into practice to be appreciated. Of course, one doesn't have to stick rigidly to correspondences – they are not intended as a doctrine. Rather they are a ladder or a framework, leading sideways, upwards, downwards and beyond and a structure with which to make sense of inner revelations which might otherwise be unsettling.

It is interesting that Qabalists use the 'Tree of Life' while Ogham uses many trees. Many shamanic cosmologies are based on cosmic trees. Witches riding their besoms has been seen as a metaphor for shamanic journeys, 'riding' a branch of the World Tree (another interpretation of witchy broomsticks!). Our Christmas tree, a mini World Tree or Tree of Life honours these associations at the rebirth time of Yule. Trees are wonderful things and it is small wonder that many people become concerned at their indiscriminate destruction, for they have meanings outside those of environmental concerns.

Mistletoe

Mistletoe has longstanding associations with Druidry. It is a parasitic plant that grows on several trees. It was mistletoe grown on the oak that Druids revered, for they saw this as deeply symbolic. Mistletoe berries are like semen, and the seeds have not touched the ground – so they represent potential. Cutting the mistletoe at Yule means enacting the moment of conception and incarnation. The mistletoe was cut with a golden sickle – a combination of Sun and Moon, masculine and feminine, drawing the divine spark down into the body. As the oak stands for tradition and form and the mistletoe for spirit, their union is full of mystical significance. The fertility symbolism of this is obvious, but to the Druids wisdom was important, and so the mistletoe would have the more esoteric meaning of the Word made Flesh. This can only be done by the union of opposites, the complementary, masculine and feminine, Sun and Earth.

Celtic paganism

Celtic myths and attitudes figure in many current pagan approaches. However, there are some pagans who seek a path that is exclusively Celtic in terminology, craft, poetry, ritual and life. The Celtic soul seems to lend itself to paganism. The Irish especially think of their history mythologically, with mythic races of the Cessair, Partholon, Nemed, Fir Bolg and Tuatha De Danaan preceeding the human Gaels. These races are described in the twelfth century Leabhar Gabhala Eireann, or Book of Invasions.

The Tuatha De Danaan (pronounced *Too-ah day Dawn-ann*) were the 'people of the Goddess Dana', the great mother goddess. They are a magical race who are part of the Irish faery folk, possessing a Cauldron of Abundance which holds the secret of life and death. The earlier Partholon fought the primitive and terrible one-eyed deities called the Fomhoire. The time of humans began when the Gaels landed on Irish soil, and their connection with the land was proclaimed by Amergin the Bard.

Many pagans today use the theme of the quartered circle as a basis for ritual and philosophy. The ancient Irish divided the sacred Land herself into four provinces, with correspondences, as follows:

Leinster: East/Life/Air/Spring/Dawn/Sword (or Arrow)
Muster: South/Light/Fire/Summer/Noon/Spear (or Rod)
Connaught: West/Love/Water/Autumn/Evening/Cauldron (or Cup)
Ulster: North/Law/Earth/Winter/Night/Stone (or Shield or Mirror)

All of the Four Elements are included here, and these are unified by Ether or Spirit. Geographically this was represented by Meath at the centre, the seat of kingship, where stood the royal halls of Tara. It is likely that ancient England, Wales and Scotland had a similar pattern.

Celts from Ireland moved to Scotland as late as the fifth century CE (Common Era) arriving in Dalriada, which is now called Argyllshire. A group of present-day Celtic pagans are named the 'clan Dalriada' and their system includes the lore of the Fir Bolg, Fomhoire, Tuatha De Danaan and the Irish Celts, celebrating light and dark and seeing everyday life as religious expression.

Celtic history is diffuse, and when we speak of the Celts we are talking about a social and linguistic grouping rather than a strictly tribal and genetic one. The Irish, Welsh and Scots have their own myths, which were transmitted orally for centuries, and these have common themes. The Celts may be thought of as emerging as a recognisable culture in Europe at around 500 BCE. The Celts were savage warriors who collected the heads of their enemies; the sentimental portrayal of them as the fey and dreamy race often favoured today is only partially true. However, heads were hunted for their power and symbology, for the Celts revered eloquence and poetry and respected the potency of the spoken word, which of course issues from the head. The spread of Celtic ways was not due to organized conquest, and indeed Celtic ways often fought each other. It seems Celtic myths, art and religion grew among and within the invaders and the invaded, and were an expression of the development of the collective consciousness of humankind.

We think of Celtic peoples as having one foot in the world of Faerie, and to some extent this is true. For instance, to my Irish father the 'little people' were as real as bread and butter. These are the people of the Sidhe (pronounced *shee*) – the dwellers in the hollow hills – and there are many folk-tales about them. Celtic people are often credited with having 'second sight' that fades when they leave their native land. However, they are great pragmatists. Their way of going about things may not be the same as the Anglo-Saxon, but they get results. Perhaps it is unease at this that gives rise to so many jokes at their expense!

Some confusion arises about Celtic races even today. Scholars divide them into two major linguistic groups, the P-Celts and the Q-Celts. Q-Celtic is found in Irish Gaelic, Scots and Manx, while P-Celtic (where the sound *q, c* and *k* are often replaced with *p*) lives on in Welsh, Breton and the remnants of the Cornish tongue. Celts of different extractions do not always like each other much. Perhaps it is uncomfortable to be comforted by something so like ourselves, yet different enough to be recognized as such. Also Celts are fiercely independent. They have been marginalized and confined but they have never been fully conquered or subsumed, and the Celtic soul paradoxically, is something that is longed for and imitated by races that have tried to subdue, mock or patronise them.

There is a great deal that is relevant to modern pagans in the old Celtic attitudes. For instance, the land was Sovereign Goddess and the King derived his power to rule from Her. If this bond was impaired or violated, sickness and wastage would ensue. This is echoed in the Arthurian myths, which are later forms of much earlier material. The Celts had a profound veneration for Place and to them the land was sacred. Wells, hilltops, trees and other natural features were considered divine. This may have contributed to their defeat by the Romans, for Celtic combat was ritualized and they would not have dreamt of carving up the countryside with earthworks designed to aid them in battle, as did the Roman legions. Today we see that instinct and mysticism are no overt match for linear logic, and yet the victory of the rational is barren – quite literally. The glory that was Rome has decayed, but the poetry and vision of the Celts is very much alive. Although fierce warriors, the Celts often decided battles by single combat. This is echoed in the tale of 'Math, Son of Mathonwy', from the collection of tales called the *Mabinogion*. King Pryderi, having been wronged by the magician Gwydion, faces him in man-to-man contest. Pryderi is slain by Gwydion's magic, but further slaughter among the armies is avoided.

The Celtic calender was constructed according to the Moon, Queen of the night-time. Just as the Celtic year began (according to some scholars) at Samhain, the start of winter, so too the Celtic day began at nightfall. Darkness was the source, the beginning, Crone came before Maiden, death was inextricably linked to life. We pay lip-service to this, but we are unwilling to accept its implications, for they are painful. Cernunnos, our Horned God, protector of the animals and the instinctual, is depicted by some writers as being linked less to sexual delight, fruitfulness and abandon, than to hunting and culling, purifying and sacrificing. We who find it hard to let go must learn from the bare winter trees, the north wind and the deep, lonely well of midnight, as the Celts did.

By a similar token, the Underworld is seen as a place of regeneration. In the Underworld was a cauldron of rebirth, from which the later Grail legends derive. The cauldron, of course, is a feminine symbol, but also has much to do with transformation, as ingredients are transformed into a brew. The goddess Cerridwen has a magical cauldron. So also does the Daghdha, the great Irish god. The Daghdha was a titanic figure, with a club that conferred life from one tip and death from the other. He is depicted in lusty mating with the death goddess, the Morrigan, at Samhain. Here the Morrigan is the 'Washer at the Ford' – the dread apparition that might be seen before battles, washing the armour of those who were to die. He has intercourse with her as she stands astride the River Unius in Connaught. So the god of Life mates with the goddess of Death. This god was often a figure of ribald fun, wearing a tunic that didn't cover his buttocks. So the strands interweave – life and death, sacred and profane, laughter and tragedy, ridicule and wonder. In thinking of the Celts we do well to bear in mind that they did not separate, split and compartmentalize. Their myth was part of their life; inner and outer were the same.

Celtic knotwork is a fascinating and beautiful decorative art. It is also symbolic of Celtic attitudes, for they saw all existence as linked – actions and reactions, life and the individual, Otherworld, Underworld, the Everyday, person, god/dess and place all intertwine in an endless web. Tweak any part, however gently, and the entire network resonates in harmony. As the Gaels land on the Irish shore, at Beltane, their bard, Amergin, delivers a beautiful pagan litany:

> I am a stag: of seven tines ...
> I am a hill: where poets walk,
> I am a boar: ruthless and red,
> I am a breaker: threatening doom ...
> I am an infant: who but I
> Peeps from the unhewn dolmen arch?

This is a many-faceted statement, but clearly the bard, the people, the animals, plants and the land, the fearsome, the beautiful, the wise and the innocent are declared as one, and celebrated. As we wear Celtic knotwork today, in jewellery, we can let out minds follow the twisting, delving path it represents, back into the magical world that was then, and that still exists.

Originally Celtic myths were preserved orally, and there were many different goddesses and gods, associated with different locations – stream, wells, grove. And yet a traveller could recognize familiar deities even though they might be called by a different name. Pantheons were not unified and unchanging. The ancient mother goddesses were terrifying as much as nurturing, and goddesses were considered more powerful than gods, from their relationships with the land. Women, too, were powerful and respected, and succession was matrilinear. Gentle pagans of today no doubt have little in common with the wild, painted and armed Celtic warrior, and yet there is so much about the Celts that speaks of what we seek now. How then do we reclaim it?

To find the Celtic soul, go to where the pewter sea shatters against scarred rock, go to where the mist spirals, to some forest place smelling of moss and secrets. Curl in the claw of a tree-root, stand on a cliff-top and face the grey sky, or listen to the many-tongued mountain stream. Go to find your goddesses and gods, don't take them with you as shapes, pre-formed and pretty, but let them speak to you out of the land.

9

the Northern Tradition

The Northern Tradition is inspired by Norse and Anglo-Saxon myth. It is dramatic and dynamic, and followers are called heathens rather than pagans. They believe it is natural to worship gods inspired by our forbears. Some people have asserted that this path is more masculine-orientated, yet there are as many goddesses as gods and these are considered equal in power. The Norse tradition is also called Asatru, after a grouping of gods called the Aesir.

The Vikings have been rather unfairly linked with rape and pillage because their activities were documented by monks, who were their victims – the equally warlike Celts may have fared better. However, Norse society included much in the way of crafts such as jewellery, poetry, a sophisticated legal system and a pioneering spirit. The bestial horned helmets were actually only ever worn for ritual purposes, reminiscent of the horned god of nature.

Deities

Norse deities are divided between the Vanir, who are nature spirits, and the more clearly defined Aesir. The faith itself is called Asatru, or Odintru, for the god Odin is its principal inspiration. The Anglo-Saxons called him Woden, and he has given his name to Wednesday. Deities are divided equally between male and female, and women had considerable status among the Norsemen, having the right, as some writers have asserted, to vote, divorce, and own land long before their modern British counterparts. Many women are currently attracted to the Norse tradition although it seems less Goddess-orientated than most other pagan paths. Followers tend to reject 'armchair heathenism' in favour of pursuing environmental initiatives, such as protecting badgers or yew trees, and involvement in national campaigns.

Runes and the Tree of Life

The runes and the image of the world ash tree, Yggdrasil, a Tree of Life symbol with nine worlds, are central to all Northern Traditions and magic. These nine worlds are as follows: Midgard, the land of ordinary mortals; Asgard, land of the Aesir; Hel, the world of the Dead; Vanaheim, home of the Vanir and Freya's Hall; the land of Fire, the land of the Light Elves, the land of the Dark Elves, the land of the Ice Giants and the land of Fog. Nine is a number of great symbolic importance in Asatru, as it was to the Celts. The runes are mystical symbols used in magic, descriptively, as an alphabet, and in divination in a way similar to the Tarot. Odin hung on the world tree, Yggdrasil, for nine days to learn the secret of the runes in a shamanic experience.

Magic, ritual and myth

There are three types of Norse magic: Seidr, intuitive, herbalistic and shamanistic, Galdr, the written and spoken ritualistic side and Taufr, which deals with talismans. The goddess Freya (goddess of love and beauty who has given her name to Friday) imparted the secrets of Seidr to Odin. Seidr is practised by the Volva, a seeress, and the Grimsrular, who are shamanic priests. There are also Gothi and Gotha – community priests and priestesses, who practise Galdr and Taufr. These are still alive within the Northern Tradition. Like most other pagan systems, rituals are adapted from other methods and suited to a modern approach. The Vikings themselves were a people who looked to the future.

Odinists usually celebrate at Full Moon and the eight seasonal festivals, but there are variations in the mythology. For instance, at Yule, which is the Norse New Year, the myth of the beautiful god Baldur is remembered. Baldur is the Sun God, who is plagued by awful dreams of death. So Freya, his mother, goes around the world getting every living thing to promise not to harm him, which they readily do, for everyone loves the Sun. The gods amuse themselves by flinging anything and everything at the now invincible Baldur. However, Loki, god of mischief, discovers that the only living thing overlooked has been the mistletoe, being too young and insignificant to cause harm. Disguised as an old woman, he whispers in the ear of poor, blind Hlod, Baldur's brother, and persuades him to join the game. He guides his hand as he flings a spear of mistletoe at Baldur, who falls down and dies.

Now the Aesir and all of creation are plunged into mourning. Odin sends to the realms of the goddess Hel, who says she will return Baldur to the upper world if everything alive cries for the Sun god. Tears fall all over the world, but the only person who refuses to cry is a grumpy old giantess, who is Loki in disguise. So Baldur must remain for ever in the land of shadows. Loki is discovered and pays a terrible penalty, chained in the bowels of the earth, while poison from a serpent drips unendingly on him. His shakes and screams are the cause of earthquakes, and so he will writhe until the end of the world.

This is a no-nonsense myth which puts us in touch with endings. Of course we know that Baldur must be born again or the Sun would never return. However, to experience death and darkness the ending must feel final, for only in this way can a transformation take place. Loki represents the necessary force of destruction, without which there can be no true change or growth – and it is interesting that he is an androgynous figure, habitually dressing up as women, who in this story are rather crone-like. In a way it seems unfair that he should suffer so badly, but his power is in no way diminished, manifesting as earthquakes and tremors which shake the foundations of all security.

Organizations

Sources for Odinists are not as plentiful as for some other traditions, being principally the Eddas, two books written in Iceland after its Christianization, plus the rune poems and other fragments. Some consider this a good thing, for Odinists are not restricted as Wiccans are, being free to be creative and inventive, within the spirit of their tradition. Also they have to think carefully about their rituals and ethics, because there are no prescribed ways to follow, which encourages independence and responsibility in the Viking tradition. Odinists organize themselves into 'hearths' or work solo. Some have a variety of ritual equipment, like Wiccans; others have little more than a candle. Some wear robes, or go sky-clad if everyone is happy this way, but many just wear their ordinary clothes. Magic is not necessarily worked, for some Odinists are happy merely to celebrate their religion. There is a preference for conducting rites outdoors in groves of trees where possible, preferably of ash, oak and hazel.

There is no system of hierarchy or degrees, just one Hearth Guardian who oversees the setting up of the group. However, there is an umbrella organization called Odinshof, a registered charity, founded in 1987, whose aims are to promote awareness of Odin's ancient teachings and philosophy. It is run by the Witan Assembly, and has several hundred members in Britain and abroad. The Witan Assembly has a grading of Odal and Oak. New members start at Odal and are promoted to Oak after 13 moons if they have proved themselves worthy and achieved experience.

10

sci-fi and psychology

We know that pagans are inspired by myths drawn from ancient times. However, some are also fired by personalities and ideas from science fiction. This is not as surprising as it may seem, for ancient gods and aliens can both be termed 'archetypal', meaning they embody principles from the Collective Unconscious. This is a deep fund of universal experience that we all share, that we sometimes enter in dreams, that we may be overwhelmed by in psychosis, and that we draw upon in states of trance and magical work. The best science fiction writers are able to draw from this well of symbolism and are able to bring mythical figures, such as Persephone, Pan, Cerridwen, and other gods, to life for us.

The psychologist C. G. Jung taught that myth was important, for mythic dramas are an allegory of what goes on in the personality. Contemplating myths is fascinating even when we don't analyse them for their relevance. They can also draw us nearer to a feeling of wholeness, which brings us closer to the divine. Sci-fi is modern myth. Although it lacks the dignity of antiquity it can be as evocative as the most ancient stories.

One of the most inspiring sci-fi novels is Robert Heinlein's *Stranger in a Strange Land* which was popular in the 1960s. It tells of an Earth boy raised on Mars by aliens. When he returns to Earth he has a deep respect for life but he is bewildered, finding it hard to understand things that most humans regard as basic. In the book, the main purpose of a Martian's life is to experience fully the entirety of things (a mystical union that is sought by many pagans). In water-brotherhood, one of the principal ceremonies, water is shared and a deep bond formed. Water is the basis of all life and widely symbolic. Water rituals, such as hand-washing, sometimes arise spontaneously in groups. Heinlein's novel still inspires the Church of All Worlds, a pagan organization founded in the 1960s in America and still going strong, with branches in Australia. One of their exhortations is 'Never thirst'. Spiritual thirst can be slaked by participation in nature, so Heinlein's novel is an account of what we seek today.

Another well-known science fiction saga is that of *Star Trek*, still alive and well in various forms after 30 years. The mission, 'To boldly go where no man has gone before', is a brave statement about the spirit of humanity. The message of respect and co-operation between nations and alien species is also attractive. *Star Trek* has a large cult following. Of course, this seems far from religion in the more accepted sense, but as we have seen, paganism is about quests, not dogma, and *Star Trek* is a quest *par excellence* 'to seek out new worlds and new civilizations'. It is the original *Star Trek* that is interesting for our purpose here, in the shape of the four main characters, Captain Kirk, Mr Spock, Dr 'Bones' McCoy and Scottie (with his engines) – all of whom have reappeared in the 2009 blockbusting *Star Trek 11* movie.

Jung and the Four Functions of Consciousness

To understand the importance of these four we need to return to Jung again and look at his concept of the Four Functions of Consciousness. These ideas have been developed and used widely, for instance in the Myers-Briggs personality test. Jung was a pioneering intellect. He made connections between ancient wisdom – practices such as alchemy – and modern analytical psychology in a way that has enabled us to build bridges between ancient and modern and value what might otherwise be dismissed as primitive or superstitious. The idea of the Four Elements (Air, Water, Fire and Earth) and their link with personality is embedded in many cultures. It corresponds with the twelve astrological signs, which divide into groups of three under each element. These are Fire (Aries, Leo, Sagittarius), Earth (Taurus, Virgo, Capricorn), Air (Gemini, Libra, Aquarius) and Water (Cancer, Scorpio, Pisces). Jung developed this idea into four basic functions of consciousness – Thinking (Air), Feeling (Water), Intuition (Fire) and Sensation (Earth).

According to Jung each individual has one or two of these functions dominant, while the others are mostly unconscious. Jung described Thinking and Feeling as 'evaluative'. Feeling in this sense does not mean strong emotion. It means evaluating in terms of humanity, family, nearest and dearest, whereas Thinking also evaluates, but by means of logic. Thinking and Feeling are polar opposites and it is hard for both to be conscious at once. A person whose dominant function is Feeling will find it hard to use logic to any great extent and will not make any major decisions on the basis of it. A Feeling person is likely to be in tune with the current mores of society and to be conscious of the reactions and feelings of other people. When called upon to say what they think, they will still say what they feel, because it will be hard to identify 'thinking'. Thinking will thus be an 'inferior' function. This doesn't mean the person doesn't think, but thought may emerge as half-baked, secondhand ideas and some surprisingly rigid and prejudiced opinions which they may adhere to stubbornly.

Someone in whom Thinking is the superior function values logic and believes people should say what they mean. Truth and reason are all-important and emotions are suspect. However, this doesn't mean the 'Thinking' type doesn't have feelings – they do – and because these are relegated to the unconscious they are often very primitive and may take the ascetic intellectual one day by storm. The sort of scenario that may illustrate this is the professor who falls desperately in love with the prostitute. The Thinking type also finds himself ambushed by inconvenient emotions in smaller ways, and may exude an inky atmosphere of jealousy, which he will strenuously deny but which everyone is aware of. Despite the labels, none of the functions has the monopoly on intelligence, for all are able to use memory and meaningful association of ideas, but in different ways.

Intuition and Sensation are another pair of opposites, and these functions Jung called 'perceptual' because they concern ways of perceiving existence, rather than evaluating. Sensation function is the reality function, for the Sensation type is rooted in the here and now and the evidence of his five senses. Sensation types often appear very sensible, but they are not necessarily logical. Intuitives, on the other hand, inhabit the world of possibilities. They are people with hunches, projecting their consciousness into the future or the past, sowing many seeds of inspiration, but rarely staying to reap. What they perceive is other realms – things that can't be put into words. But that doesn't mean they are necessarily airy-fairy or ineffectual. If they have the courage of their convictions they are very dynamic, and may be directors of successful companies or players on the stockmarket. It is possible to have more than one function operating efficiently, and by mid-life most people work with two or three. Becoming a totally balanced person means having access to all four – although none of these ideas is set in tablets of stone.

The idea of the four elements/functions can be called 'archetypal' and so holds unending fascination. It turns up in astrology as Fire, Earth, Air and Water, and shows in figures of gods and goddesses, many of whom embody a particular element. Lugh, for example, is a fire god, connected to dying and resurrecting as flames do, as the Sun does, as the inspiration of intuitive people comes and goes.

Returning to *Star Trek*, where the four functions are so neatly embodied, the most obvious has to be Spock as the Thinker – ever logical and controlled. And with whom is he always arguing? With the Feeling Doctor, of course, who values human life and relationships. Kirk is the Intuitive captain, making split-second decisions on the basis of his hunches, and Scottie, with his engines, is the Sensation type, keeping the practicalities running smoothly.

This may all sound like a game – and a geekie one at that! – but it is useful. Inexorably we are fascinated by our opposite. Thinking types are drawn to Feeling people, Intuitives to Sensation function, and thereby often hangs a tale of misery, frustration, incomprehension and heartache. It can be like living with an alien, and it can be so hard to realize that this person really does see the world totally differently, is both scared by and attracted to what you represent and really can't help it. And the same is true of you.

Thinking and Feeling types can have a difficult time. Thinker can't understand why Feeler is so illogical and uncontrolled – yet he longs to bask in that warmth of feeling. And Feeler can't understand why Thinker is so cold and unsympathetic – yet she longs for some of that detachment. Intuition and Sensation, being perceptual rather than evaluative, don't have such a hard time, for they are more prone to let the other get on with it, walking hand in hand and parallel (on a good day!).

To determine which is your uppermost function it is sometimes easiest to consider what you can't do. Can't work keys, tools, objects, bewildered by car and kitchen – then you may be an Intuitive. Can't bear displays of emotion, want everything to be clear-cut and organized – then you are probably a Thinker. Can't see the point of logic, it's cold, a dead-end and you feel misunderstood – then perhaps you're a Feeling type. Feel mystified and suspicious about magic and the non-rational, and impatient with 'airy-fairy' people – then you may be a Sensation type. Your astrological sign is some indication, and some astrologers equate Fire with Intuition, Water with Feeling, Air with Thinking and Earth with Sensation but this is very general.

You may have noticed that I've used 'he' mainly for Thinking and 'she' for Feeling, because that seems to be more often than not the way it is, but certainly it is not always so. Also you may notice that Thinking and Sensation have been valued by our culture, which is materialistic and scientifically logical, whereas the other functions are regarded with suspicion, or worse. Thus Intuitive and Feeling people may be more likely than others to try to develop other sides to themselves, to gain acceptance. However, paganism is about balance. The purpose of finding our inferior function is so we can develop it and understand better. Often the way to the divine is connected to the inferior function, and represented in fairy-tales and stories by a helpful animal or seemingly foolish or damaged person who leads the way to the 'happy ever after'. If you are fascinated by things that belong to your 'inferior' side, so much better, for there lies true knowledge and magic.

An important part of many pagan rituals involves calling on the four quarters, North, South, East and West. North corresponds to Earth, East to Air, South to Fire and West to Water. These are the protective and powerful elements that make up our reality. They also link in with the four forces within the human being, Sensation, Thinking, Intuition and Feeling. So inner and outer are linked. Entry into the ancient mystery cult of Eleusis involved the injunction 'Know thyself'. That is not easy, but it is something that many pagans are concerned with, at least to some degree. Paganism is hardly about self-analysis, although many pagans are healers, counsellors or psychotherapists of some sort. Covens and hearths are not encounter groups. However, paganism is about self-realization and spiritual development, and wholeness is part of this process. Thinking about how our minds work can be a great help in understanding life in general and acquiring inner balance.

Jung put forward many ideas relevant to anyone on an esoteric path. For instance, his concept of the Shadow is very important. The Shadow is composed of the parts of us that are not conscious. It is the Dweller on the Threshold and it is one of the first things you meet when becoming involved in magic and trance. It is important to identify the Shadow as far as possible, for you won't be able to keep it out of your magic circle however much you sweep and banish. If you are sure you have 'risen above' it think again, because you may be deluding yourself. Contrary to popular belief, the Shadow may contain desirable as well as undesirable things. It may hold power and talent – things we have kept at bay to make ourselves more acceptable. Starhawk, in her chapter on Trance in *The Spiral Dance* (Harper & Row, 1989) has valuable things to say on this subject.

Jung also tells us about the animus and anima: the 'inner man' for women and the 'inner woman' for men, respectively. Offering feminine ideas of the divine as well as masculine, paganism explores ways of understanding and relating to these parts of ourselves. None of these concepts are rigid, and they have been much developed and explored by more recent analytical psychologists.

11

paganism in daily life

Love for the Earth is part of the pagan soul. We take from the bounty of the Earth gladly, and give back with equal pleasure. If paganism is a way of life, then that way of life needs to take into account the welfare of all creatures on Earth, and of the Earth herself. Green spirituality is so much a part of true paganism that it hardly needs to be stated. It also seems to be common sense and sound survival instinct.

In *Gaia* (Oxford, 1987), J. E. Lovelock writes: 'It does not seem inconsistent with the Darwinian forces of evolutionary selection for a sense of pleasure to reward us by encouraging us to achieve a balanced relationship between ourselves and other forms of life.' In other words, he is saying that loving nature is a survival instinct. However, it is one that we have almost lost, suppressed by worship of science and the urge to 'progress'. Many pagans are passionate about nature, and have risked life and limb to protect areas of beauty from the bulldozer. Others are much more laid back, but a devotion to the Earth is always present.

Trees arouse many feelings in sensitive people, who have fought to preserve them. They are heavy with symbolism, as in the Tree of Life, the World Tree and in the ancient Ogham alphabet. They are beautiful as poised dancers over hill and valley, and they are useful for their wood, fruits and their contribution to the atmosphere. But they are something much more, something that we cannot fully encompass. Pagans express their love and respect for trees by asking the tree if they may cut a branch, and thanking it afterwards. Of course, if you ask you must listen with your inner ear for the answer. This may seem crazy, but what is actually taking place is a harmonizing of the human with the tree, and the act of asking the tree opens the intuition.

It is often unclear exactly what is harmful to the environment and what isn't. Scientists argue, and are sometimes suspected of leaning towards views that support whoever happens to be paying them. Emotions run high among environmental pressure groups, who cannot bear to see another slice of hillside carved up, or another river polluted beyond all recognition. This may not always be reasonable, but it is understandable. Perhaps what we are needing to salvage is something in ourselves as much as nature – that wild and free spirit, of which civilization and the de-souling of nature has robbed us.

The Earth has withstood many huge changes in her lifetime and none of these have destroyed her – although sometimes many life-forms perished during climatic adjustments. Probably the worst harm we can do would be to render this beautiful world uninhabitable by us and many other species but Gaia would survive. J. E. Lovelock has put forward a reasoned argument for considering the Earth sentient and self-regulating, which he says country people have always known. In some ways anything we do is 'natural' for we are children of Gaia. In another sense even living is unfriendly to the environment, for we all produce methane – a greenhouse gas – along with many other polluting qualities of our bodies. So what on earth do we do?

As usual the answer is probably one of balance. We should not decide to stop living as we know it, give up all the comforts of civilization and return to tribal ways – we could hardly do this even if we wanted to. However, we should proceed with respect and common sense, and with awareness attempt an attunement with our mother the Earth. We probably need our instincts as much as anything else for this, for years of environmental science have supplied few definite answers. However, this is as much a matter of our spiritual well-being as our physical, for unless we respect the Earth we cannot properly respect ourselves or our fellows. A little true deference for nature will do more than pages of equations and formulae.

However, practical measures are not the whole story, for many pagans perform eco-magic. These are rituals for general Earth healing, or for specific environmental or humanitarian causes. The energy of the Earth that we discussed in Chapter 2 may be raised and focused to the objective in question. This is done responsibly and positively, for the object is to help the Earth and the life upon her, not to harm the polluters.

Technology

If Gaia is a living, sentient creature, then we who are part of her have a function within her system. Lovelock suggests that mankind may be a 'Gaian nervous system' and a part of her development: through us she can reach into space, through us she can become conscious of herself, and through us she may have a chance to survive the type of event that could otherwise devastate her – for example a collision with a meteor. Our advancing technology might prevent this as nothing else could, providing, for example, perhaps the only imaginable positive use of the atom bomb.

Technology is certainly not all harmful, although pagans can be divided on this subject. Some favour the 'back-to-nature' approach, but there are some who tried it and found it can be uncomfortable and joyless. Some are suspicious of technology, but others embrace it as being very much in keeping with a world-view that gives room to all possibilities, and see computers as a type of magic. Computers are very much part of life. Love them or hate them – and it is characteristic of pagans to do either or both – they are part of the lives of most people.

Computers do offer something positive environmentally: they are clean and use very little power. Making full use of computers does not have to take anything away from spending time with nature, and appreciating it. There is a special place for computers in a world wishing to retrieve community values, to save energy and to encourage communication and cross-fertilization between groups and nations. The Internet has been brilliant for pagans wishing to communicate and find support, information and kindred spirits, and it may also have contributed to greater acceptance of pagan paths.

In addition to the practical benefits of the information superhighway, some occultists perceive this as something greater than the sum of its parts – a change in and a step up for the energies of the planet, a force for alteration in consciousness. It is widely believed that we are entering the Age of Aquarius. Aquarius is ruled by Uranus, the planet of electricity, of invention and innovation. All these are exemplified by the World Wide Web.

Witches are weavers, and if we are wise we weave into the tapestry of life without pulling threads. Celtic knotwork is an artistic expression of the intricacies of the web of life, the many interconnections, the pattern of existence, death, rebirth – the continuing thread. In some strange way the Internet, the web of energy and communication around the globe into which anyone who can get to a terminal can 'sew a thread', partakes of these concepts. It is an abstract that we have access to, but which we can never completely encompass at any one time. It is a creation of science, yet it is something more. It offers us a possible expansion of experience, of new dimensions, even though much of what is available on the Net may be essentially trivial.

So there are plenty of 'cyber-pagans' – those who are very well attuned to the possibilities offered by computers and the information superhighway as well as the old, deep energies of Mother Earth. Like the Roman god Janus (who gave his name to January) we need to have two faces – one that looks backwards to our ancient past, and another that looks forwards to a New Age that isn't 'just crystals and light' but is the real dawning of a new consciousness. Maybe we can complete the circle. Having left our roots, our instincts and tribal ways to develop a sense of logic, reason and science, perhaps we can now reconnect with these roots: not rejecting all we have learned along the way, but respecting intuition and a sense of origin and combining it to use the best our science has produced – in a sense to come back to our place of origin and to know it for the first time. Then we will truly have a New Age – an inspiring thought!

Practice

Stand outside in the sunshine. Let the warmth fall upon you, within you. Feel the glow gathering in power and warmth behind your navel. When you are ready hold out your arms and let the healing energies flow outwards. Visualize them healing the Earth, revitalizing the soil. Imagine this clearly, then let go. You may do the same on a windy day, taking a deep breath of the wild air and breathing out, imagining the wind sweeping away all harm. Similarly with rain, if you don't mind getting wet. Imagine the cleansing energies of the rainwater taking away pollutants, beautifying the land. These small rituals will be more effective if undertaken at a place that is special to you, or at a well, near a standing stone or in a place of beauty.

Say a pagan grace at important meals. You could simply say, 'I thank everything that gives its life to feed mine, and the Earth for nourishing me.'

Take the time to contact trees, lean on them, sit by them and absorb them. If you sit quietly and calmly you will feel the essence of the tree, you may see pictures with your mind's eye or have a sense of 'knowing'. Keep a note of whatever you sense, for it will be very special. Who cares about the hug-a-tree clichés – it works!

Enjoy the Earth, walk on her, breathe the air, touch the trees, and let your instincts tell you the way to live in harmony with her.

Taking things further

Becoming a pagan requires no specific action. If you feel that path is right for you then you are on it, and all you have to do is to explore and develop at your own pace. A good place to start is by observing the eight seasonal festivals in whatever way you like, maybe simply by going for a walk and lighting a candle. Keep a notebook of your experiences, because they will unfold week after week, year after year.

If you want a more formal or specific commitment, perhaps to Wicca or Druidry, then the best place to start is with the Pagan Federation, who will be able to put you in touch with local coordinators and groups. You should obviously always be careful about any new contacts, especially if you are young, because there will always be those who seek to exploit those who are inexperienced or too trusting. In particular, please bear in mind that such things as training and initiation should never be offered in exchange for sex.

Resources on the Internet are endless. You may like to start by logging on to:

www.paganfed.org/

The Pagan Federation also produce a print magazine called *Pagan Dawn*.